Fated to Pretend?:

Culture Crisis and the Fate of the Individual

by

Rebecca Jade Ok

A thesis submitted in partial fulfillment of the
requirements for the degree of

Master of Arts
in
Political Science

Thesis Committee:
Craig Carr, Chair
David Kinsella
Birol Yeşilada

Portland State University
2013

## ABSTRACT

The question of this thesis is whether the individual can resolve the problem of culture crisis in her own case. Culture crisis is a historical moment in which our culture leads us to expect a world drastically different from the one in which we find ourselves. This thesis will focus on the experience of Generation Y in the fall-out of the 2008 Recession. It will be argued that we need a Wittgensteinian view of language in order to account for the phenomenon of culture crisis. It will be suggested that our individual has to be a Nietzschean individual in order to resolve the problem of culture crisis in her own case. Potential incompatibilities between a Wittgensteinian view of language and the Nietzschean individual will be considered and rejected. It will be concluded that in order to resolve the problem of culture crisis in her own case the individual must change the way she lives.

ACKNOWLEDGEMENTS

I would like to thank Professor Carr for re-igniting my curiosity and allowing me the freedom to see where it would take me, Andrei for his unending encouragement, Portland State University for providing the opportunity and financial support necessary to pursue this research, and the University of Oxford for allowing me to make use of its superior resources.

CONTENTS

# PREFACE

I'm feeling rough, I'm feeling raw, I'm in the prime of my life.
Let's make some music, make some money, find some models for wives.
I'll move to Paris, shoot some heroin, and fuck with the stars.
You man the island and the cocaine and the elegant cars.

This is our decision, to live fast and die young.
We've got the vision, now let's have some fun.
Yeah, it's overwhelming, but what else can we do.
Get jobs in offices, and wake up for the morning commute.

. . .

There's really nothing, nothing we can do
Love must be forgotten, life can always start up anew.
The models will have children, we'll get a divorce
We'll find some more models, everything must run its course.

We'll choke on our vomit and that will be the end
We were fated to pretend
To pretend
We're fated to pretend
To pretend[1]

---

[1]MGMT (2008)

INTRODUCTION

On October 3, 2008 newspapers across the nation were splashed with headlines announcing the $700 billion bank bailout. Coverage discussed failures in regulatory oversight and the ethical shortcomings of the finance industry. In the weeks and months following the announcement of the bailout, newspapers were heavy with stories of the collapse of the housing market, mass lay-offs, and numerous individuals who had become homeless essentially overnight.

Nearly five years later the discussion of the effects of the Recession has turned its attention to Generation Y. By and large the members of Generation Y find themselves unable to build the kind of life they were taught to expect. Many of the members of Generation Y are unable to find a job that pays a living wage. They are burdened with tens of thousands of dollars of student loan debt. They are unable to purchase cars, afford to get married or have children. In short, Generation Y entered the workforce and were immediately forced to put their lives on hold.

Despite these set backs the members of Generation Y remain optimistic. Surveys show that a majority of Generation Y believes they will be able to achieve the kind of life and degree of success they want. These numbers hold even amongst those who moved back in with their parents after graduating college or working for a few years.

The question is whether this optimism will prove prescient or foolish. Numerous forecasts suggest that Generation Y will be the first generation since the

Depression that is worse off than their parents. Jobs reports show that the economy is consistently adding jobs. However, a closer look shows that these jobs are
low-salary jobs rather than the mid-salary jobs that fund a middle-class life. The
combination of the growing wealth gap and the pressures of globalization indicate
that Generation Y's optimism may be unfounded.

Many members of Generation Y are lightly revising their idea of the good
life. They wait a few more years to get married and have children. They rent or buy
small condos or houses in urban centers. They prefer living in dense, multi-use areas
so they can bike or walk where they need and forego car ownership altogether.

Such alterations, importantly, do not question the essential features or general
outline of the idea of the good life. Rather, they take for granted that the economy
just needs a few years to bounce back or that the individual just needs a few more
years to accumulate the necessary capital. These eventualities may not happen. As
such, continuing to be guided by an idea of the good life, but finding themselves
unable to attain it, the members of Generation Y may find themselves fated to live
unsatisfied and unfulfilling lives.

The immediate cause of this problem is economic in nature. However, the
aim of this thesis is to suggest that the problem itself is cultural. More specifically,
the problem is that the picture of the good life embedded in our political culture
is no longer attainable. In a post-Recession world, this picture only sets up the
individual for a life of dissatisfaction and failure. The problem is that the members
of Generation Y were given a picture of the good life that does not fit the post-
Recession world in which they find themselves.

Throughout this thesis I refer to this kind of phenomenon as "culture crisis."
By "culture crisis," I mean a moment in time in which our concepts do not fit the

world in which we find ourselves. In the case of Generation Y, their picture of the good life does not fit the post-Recession world. Other examples of culture crisis-inducing events might include the Great Depression, World War II, and the Vietnam War. Each of these events fundamentally challenged our ideas of how the world is, what we can expect from others, or how we can expect our lives to go. Though there are other examples of culture crisis, I will focus on the experience of Generation Y as it is contemporaneous with the writing of this thesis.

The phenomenon of culture crisis presents a particular challenge. The immediate cause of the culture crisis facing Generation Y was economic in nature. This problem is political insofar as it concerns our political culture. Moreover, it has had political repercussions both in the form of the global #Occupy movement and as one of the defining issues of the 2012 presidential election. However, an instance of culture crisis can be solved by neither economic or political means. Culture crisis can only be solved by means of a change in culture.

This presents a problem for the individual. Culture is a collective creation. It tends to change at a very slow, even evolutionary pace. But the individual members of Generation Y have lives to live right now. If they are to have any chance of living satisfied and fulfilled lives, these individuals will have to resolve the problem of culture crisis in their own case as soon as possible. They have to be able to free themselves of the pre-Recession picture of the good life and give themselves a picture better suited to the post-Recession world. The question of this thesis is whether this solution is conceptually possible.

## CULTURE CRISIS

In his acceptance speech at the 2012 Democratic National Convention, President Obama told voters that they faced a clear choice between two fundamentally different visions for the future of America. He told us that we, as Americans "insist on personal responsibility, and we celebrate individual initiative." We celebrate the individual and their achievements, but we do so with the recognition that "we have responsibilities as well as rights; that our destinies are bound together." America, President Obama insisted, is not about what I can do, or what the government can do for us, but rather "what can be done by us, together." According to President Obama, America is a place where ambitious and innovative individuals come together to achieve—together—and where the government is a means of pursuing this goal.

Governor Romney's acceptance speech at the 2012 Republican National Convention painted a different picture of America. The individual was a theme of Governor Romney's speech as well, but the idea of government as a means of pursuing collective goals was absent. In place of government, Governor Romney invoked family, church, community, and business. He held up the worker who, upon losing a well-paying full-time job with benefits, took two lower-paying jobs with fewer benefits in order to support her family as a paragon of the hard-working, heroic American. He appealed to the voter to consider whether she and her family were better off than they had been four years ago, implying that the government was responsible for the continuing fall-out of the 2008 Recession. According to Governor Romney, America is a collection of hard-working individuals who find whatever support, comfort, or redress they may need in local, non-governmental associations.

Political rhetoric aside, President Obama was right. The candidates in the 2012 presidential election represented two different visions of America. It would be a mistake, however, to think that these conflicting visions originated with the 2012 presidential election or that via the election the American public decided on one vision over the other. The passion and enthusiasm displayed by both sides during the campaign, as well as a look at the popular election results, shows a highly divided American public. President Obama may have won the office, but the American public as a whole has not adopted his vision.

In emphasizing the differences between their visions for America, President Obama and Governor Romney ignored the commonalities that underlie those visions. Talking about similarities is hardly the point of an election campaign. However, while differences may be what wins an election, examining what unites us will help us to understand the appeal of these visions and also why the American public is so divided about them. This chapter will undertake such an examination. It will acquaint the reader with the notion of political culture, develop the idea that political culture changes over time, and suggest that America is in the midst of such a change. The chapter will end by introducing the problem that will be the focus of this thesis.

## WHAT IS POLITICAL CULTURE?

What President Obama and Governor Romney neglected to tell the American public is that we are united by our political culture. "Political culture" is a term used by political theorists and scientists to refer to the shared norms and beliefs that make a group of people into a political unit. In the case of the presidential election, the political culture of interest was that set of norms and beliefs shared by the people of the United States. However, we can also speak of political culture at different levels and in different places. For instance, the state of New Hampshire has a different political culture than the state of California or Oregon. As these states belong to the same larger political unit, their respective political cultures will be similar, but there are enough differences among them that we might profitably compare and contrast them.

The shared norms and beliefs that characterize a political culture consist of some of the most basic values and assumptions we employ in our everyday lives. Political culture limits the kinds of political institutions we find acceptable. It informs how we think of ourselves and others. It shapes how we think others should be treated and how we would like to be treated ourselves. Political culture even provides a minimal picture of the good life. In providing our basic idea of what a person is it also, thereby, provides a basic idea of what constitutes a good and desirable life.[2] Political culture, then, is fundamental to our sense of ourselves as Americans and individuals. Moreover, understanding our political culture is fundamental to understanding ourselves as Americans and individuals.

Though many of us may be unfamiliar with the notion of political culture, we are all familiar with the features of our own. We believe that individuals are inherently valuable and the basic unit of society. We believe individuals are capable of making their own decisions, setting their own goals, and determining the course of their own lives, and we believe they should be treated as such. We believe that

---

[2]This is a controversial claim. The debate between moral liberals and political liberals concerns the extent to which liberal political culture has moral or normative content. I'm taking for granted here that political culture has some minimum of normative content. I think the descriptive features of a concept come with complementary normative features. That is, what a thing is tells us how it ought to be treated. If the liberal concept of "person" includes the characteristic of "inherently valuable individual capable of setting her own goals and determining the course of her own life" then we ought to treat persons as such.

all persons are equal and should be treated equally. We believe that all persons have certain rights, including the right to property, and that these rights should be protected. It is these shared norms and beliefs that unite us as Americans.

## ARE THE TIMES A-CHANGIN'?

It is a commonplace that the United States is a liberal country. It is also widely assumed that the United States has always been a liberal country. However, just as political culture can vary between different places, it can also vary between different times. When Alexis de Tocqueville, a French aristocrat and political sociologist, came to the United States in 1831 to examine democracy, he witnessed a very different country than the one we know today. There were the obvious differences: the frontier had yet to be settled, slavery was still practiced, women and African Americans were not allowed to vote. However, taking Tocqueville's account as more or less accurate reveals that the United States was at that time characterized by a republican political culture. It was precisely this republican political culture, what Tocqueville referred to as our "mores," that he thought kept the dangers of democracy and a potential power grab by the federal government at bay.[3]

One explanation of America's transformation from a republican to a liberal country has been suggested by Frederick Turner. In his *Significance of the Frontier in American History*, Turner advances what has come to be referred to as the "Turner Frontier Thesis." According to the thesis, the United States became a liberal country as a result of its confrontation with the frontier. In expanding into and settling the frontier Americans left behind social ties, community, and politics. In their place grew the increased sense of self-reliance and individualism that characterizes

---

[3]de Tocqueville (1969), 287, 397.

American political culture today.

The Frontier Thesis finds some support in Tocqueville's study of America. Though Tocqueville emphasizes the republican nature of American political culture, the careful reader will notice that he holds up New England as the exemplar region. In contrast to New England, Tocqueville is less impressed by the Western and Southwestern regions. He finds the people there less educated, less in the grip of the republican mores he identifies, and he is appalled by their elected representatives.[4] Nonetheless, Tocqueville seems confident that the Western and Southwestern regions will come to resemble New England more and more as they develop.[5] The pioneer, as Tocqueville sees him, is a man bringing civilization and democracy to the wilderness.[6] He is certain (or perhaps hopeful) that the resemblance will not be the other way around. However, if the Frontier Thesis is correct, Tocqueville simply and understandably underestimated the influence the confrontation with the frontier would have on American political culture.

According to the Frontier Thesis, then, a republican America plunged into the frontier and a liberal America came out the other side. This liberal political culture has shaped our identity, our society, and our political life. But this isn't the end of the story of American political culture. On the contrary, Craig Carr in his *Polity* suggests that we are currently facing political challenges that will have a potentially fundamental effect on our political culture. How extreme the change is, Carr warns, is up to us.

Carr identifies the source of this change in the increasingly intricate problems we need government to address. Whereas Tocqueville came to the United States to

---

[4]de Tocqueville (1969), 200.
[5]de Tocqueville (1969), 308.
[6]de Tocqueville (1969), 302-303.

study democracy, Carr argues that the functions we need government to perform nowadays are so numerous and complicated that a government substantially resembling democracy in its ideal form is simply not up to the task.[7] Rather, out of political necessity we will need to turn to the bureau as the most efficient means of dealing with our "large-scale social problems."[8] Carr refers to this as the "bureaucratic phenomenon."[9]

The bureaucratic phenomenon foreshadows a shift in our political culture. Initially, this shift will be due to an inherent tension between American liberal political culture and the nature of the bureau as an organizational structure. The source of this tension is Americans' fervent, almost religious celebration of the individual. Carr refers to this as the "myth of radical individualism."[10] We value individuals who are self-made, who play by their own rules, and control events around them. Carr describes this as a "myth" to emphasize the fact that it doesn't correspond to reality. No individual is truly self-made. What an individual manages to accomplish in her life is largely determined by the circumstances in which she finds herself.[11] Due to our radical individualism, we celebrate non-conformity as valuable in and of itself. But non-conformity does not work within the structure of the bureau. A bureau has a central task that is pursued collectively by the individuals who make it up. There's no room for playing by your own rules in the bureau.

Despite this initial tension, the bureau as an organizational structure is not

---

[7]Carr (2007), 150, 179-199.

[8]Carr (2007), 154, 159.

[9]Carr (2007), 154.

[10]Carr (2007), 205.

[11]This myth, incidentally, was nicely reflected in the 2012 Republican National Convention slogan "We built it."

inherently at odds with liberal political culture. Carr argues that our radical individualism has simply been tacked onto liberal political culture in the United States.[12] He notes that historically American political culture has predisposed us to favor decentralized, libertarian forms of government. However, he argues that such forms of government are not the only ones consistent with liberal political culture.[13] Further, decentralized forms of government are no longer adequate to effectively address the large-scale social problems of today. The turn to the bureau means, one way or another, we will have to abandon our radical individualism.

The structure of the bureau is not inherently at odds with liberal political culture. However, the bureau comes with its own culture which is. The basic assumptions and values of bureaucratic culture are inconsistent with those of liberal political culture.[14] Whereas liberal political culture takes the individual to be the basic unit of society, bureaucratic culture takes the organization to be the basic unit. Whereas liberal political culture is egalitarian, bureaucratic culture is inegalitarian and hierarchical. Whereas liberal political culture believes individuals have inherent value and their identity is theirs to determine, bureaucratic culture believes the value and identity of an individual is determined by their role within the organization.[15] Carr prescribes greater popular working knowledge of our political culture to prevent it being replaced by the antithetical bureaucratic culture. Barring such an awakening among the American public, however, the bureaucratic phenomenon means we are in for a radical shift in political culture.

Faced with such a prospect, the temptation is to suggest that we ditch the bureau. Afterall, our political culture shapes our identities and values. Surely that's

---

[12]Carr (2007), 205.
[13]Carr (2007), 96-97.
[14]Carr (2007), 207.
[15]Carr (2007), 169-174.

more important than any problem we might need to address? But Carr argues there's no stopping increasing centralization and bureaucratization. Bureaucracies have a tendency to grow even if their function does not change.[16] Bureaucracies may also simply adopt new functions, as Carr illustrates with the example of the history of the FBI.[17] Bureaucracies, once created, either grow or stay the same, but they don't go away. Moreover, there's no avoiding centralization and bureaucratization. Carr refers to this as the "centralization paradox." According to the centralization paradox, decentralized behavior requires centralization in order to manage the externalities created and the more decentralized behavior, the more centralization is needed.[18] Centralization begets more centralization and decentralization begets centralization, as well.

Carr's suggestion that we are headed for a shift in political culture instigated by the necessity of the bureau is borne out by the 2012 presidential election. President Obama's and Governor Romney's respective visions of America are simply two responses to the bureaucratic phenomenon. Governor Romney's small government vision of America reflects our continued fascination with libertarian-type forms of government. President Obama's vision, on the other hand, reflects a setting aside of radical individualism and an attempt to harness the power of the bureau to address our large-scale social problems. The debate between President Obama and Governor Romney, then, comes down to whether our historic, liberal insistence on individual self-sufficiency and decentralization is adequate to meet the needs of today or whether we can both adopt the bureau and retain our political culture, our values, and national identity.

---

[16]Carr (2007), 159.
[17]Carr (2007), 165-166.
[18]Carr (2007), 96-97.

Carr's suggestion also explains the passion and enthusiasm exhibited by the American public during the election. The two visions get to the very heart of what it means to be American. They recommend different ideas of acceptable political institutions. They offer different visions of how we might think of ourselves and each other. They offer different visions of the kinds of lives we should desire. The fact that the popular vote was fairly evenly split, however, indicates that we haven't reached consensus on how we feel about the bureau or whether we're ready to give up our radical individualism. This cultural upheaval augurs political and social upheaval, as well as uncertainty about the very basic questions political culture typically answers for us.

## POP CULTURE AND POLITICAL CULTURE

Changes in political culture tend to go unnoticed. It's not a topic about which the general public frequently thinks or talks directly. Additionally, such changes tend to happen over long periods of time and typically as the result of some other process or event, for example, settling the frontier or bureaucratization.[19] However, there is a place we can look for some indication of such changes. Remember that political culture shapes how we think about ourselves and each other and the kind of life we want to lead. As such, pop culture is a good source of insight into political culture. In television, film, music, art, and fiction we tell stories to ourselves about ourselves. These stories reflect the basic assumptions and values of their time. By focusing on certain tropes, such as what counts as a good or worthwhile person, what kind of life is portrayed as desirable, and how the characters interact with each other and various institutions we can come to some tentative conclusions about the political

---

[19]Carr (2007), 218-219.

culture of the time.

Carr engages in such pop culture analysis to trace the development of the American obsession with the radical individual and its eventual conflict with the bureau. He takes us back to the frontier and reintroduces us to such characters as Kit Carsen and Davy Crockett. These were real individuals, helping to tame the frontier away from society and the force of law with nothing but their wits and their guns standing between them and death. Romanticized stories of their adventures incited Americans' radical individualism.[20]

As Carr shows, the hero of the Old West did not ride into the sunset when the frontier was conquered. The same character re-appears time and again. The unattached, self-determining, rude, lawless—or as Carr prefers "ungovernable"— master of events continues to fascinate us. Carr cites such characters as Rick Blaine, Sam Spade, and Randall Patrick McMurphy.[21] But the story changes with McMurphy. In *One Flew Over the Cuckoo's Nest*, the bureau arises in the form of the ward and Big Nurse. The reader and the chronics cheer for McMurphy, but in the end McMurphy is "cured" by the bureau via lobotomy.[22]

There's a wrenching tragedy reflected in this pop culture analysis. Americans continue to celebrate the radical individual. We continue to hold up characters like Davy Crockett and Rick Blaine as exemplars of what a good and worthwhile individual is. And yet, the America in which we find ourselves is not a place in which such characters are appropriate. Our increasingly bureaucratized society has no room for such ungovernable individuals as McMurphy's fate at the hands of

---

[20]Carr (2007), 214-216.
[21]Carr (2007), 211, 214, 217.
[22]Carr (2007), 215-218.

Big Nurse illustrates. Rather than the Old West, we find ourselves in the cubicle-filled world of Dilbert.[23] Yet, we continue to tell ourselves stories of these mythic individuals.

Carr's pop culture analysis indicates that the conflict between our political culture and the bureau is building. Rather than coming to terms with the bureau, the suggestion is that Americans continue to cling tightly to their radical individualism. As was discussed in the previous section, there is no stopping the increasing centralization and bureaucratization of our society. The bureau will continue to rise. If Americans continue to cling to the myth of radical individualism, their political culture will increasingly be unable to make sense of the world in which they find themselves. Expecting a life of the likes of Davy Crockett or Rick Blaine, yet finding themselves in the world of Dilbert, Americans can expect to go through life either deluded or disappointed.[24]

It's reasonable to ask whether this dissonance between political culture and the practical realities of life continues to be reflected in the pop culture of today. After all, *One Flew Over the Cuckoo's Nest* was published in 1962—over fifty years ago. The comic strip Dilbert first appeared in 1989—almost twenty-five years ago. Of course, this comic still appears in newspapers and on office doors and cubicle walls everywhere. Nonetheless, twenty-five years is a considerable amount of time for pop culture. An examination of some more recent pop culture may be helpful in drawing conclusions about where we are today on reconciling ourselves to the bureau.

To this end, two sets of pop culture items will be examined. The first consists of three highly popular films from 1999. The films are The Matrix, Office Space, and Fight Club. The second consists of three highly popular television programs that

---

[23]Carr (2007), 218.
[24]Carr (2007), 218.

started airing in 2009 and continue to air new episodes at the time of writing. The shows are Community, Archer, and Parks and Recreation.

All three of the films center on a single main character. In The Matrix, this character is Thomas Anderson who later comes to be known as "Neo." In Office Space we have Peter Gibbons. In Fight Club, the main character is nameless, but toward the end of the film we learn that his partner in crime, Tyler Durden, is his alter ego. Each of these characters is a white-collar worker of some sort. Both Neo and Peter work as computer programmers while Tyler assesses liability for manufacturing flaws for a car company.

The plot of each of these films is driven by some sort of rebellion against the bureau and its demands. Perhaps the most playful of the bunch is Office Space. Peter hates his job. He hates the people he works with and his boss's drive-by, passive aggressive, wearying management style has become a cultural meme. As a result of a hypno therapy mis-hap, Peter becomes highly relaxed and through the rest of the film we see him slowly dismantle his white-collar life-style. He stops going into work regularly. When he does go into the office it's to deconstruct his cubicle, gut fish, or steal the perpetually malfunctioning printer which he and his friends destroy in one of the more cathartic scenes of the film. When his friends are down-sized in a restructuring, they upload a virus to the office computer system to steal easily over-looked fractions of pennies as revenge. A coding error, however, means the stolen amount is much larger than expected. Before Peter can return the funds, a disgruntled co-worker sets fire to the building, destroying any evidence of the theft. The film ends with a shot of a smiling Peter, now working in construction, declining his friends' offer to get him a job at their new office.

Fight Club is a darker film than Office Space. The film opens with the main character flying from one city to another on business, unable to sleep. On one of these flights the main character meets Tyler Durden. Returning home after yet another business trip the main character finds his apartment has been bombed out. He calls Tyler Durden. They agree the main character should stay at Tyler's place and then Tyler asks the main character to hit him as hard as he can. The main character also hates his boss's passive aggressive management style. Having been called into his boss's office to discuss his behavior, the main character beats himself up and blackmails his boss into keeping him on the payroll. Meanwhile, Tyler has been establishing underground fight clubs in cities all over the country and creates an organization called "Project Mayhem," which engages in anti-corporate acts of sabotage. Towards the end of the film the main character discovers Tyler's plot to bomb the office buildings of every bank in the area in order to "erase the debt... go back to zero." In his failed attempt to thwart the plan, the main character discovers that Tyler Durden is his alter ego. The film ends with Tyler on a rooftop, watching as a dozen office buildings collapse.

The Matrix is a science fiction take on the same themes as Office Space and Fight Club. Thomas Anderson is a computer programmer who spends his nights hacking. In the course of hacking he comes across references to the Matrix. He is contacted by a man named Morpheus who tells him that intelligent machines have enslaved the human race to use as a source of bioelectricity. The Matrix, Morpheus explains, is a simulation of the world as it was in 1999 that the machines use to keep the humans under control. Morpheus and his crew unplug Thomas Anderson, now known as "Neo," from the Matrix and train him to "free his mind" and manipulate the rules of the Matrix. We learn that Morpheus believes Neo is "The One," a prophesied individual with the ability to control the Matrix, defeat the machines' agents, and free humankind from their enslavement. In an encounter with an agent, Neo discovers his ability to control the Matrix and the film closes with him telling the machines that he will show humankind "a world where anything is possible."

These films indicate that circa the new millennium Americans still had not come to terms with the bureau. Each film shows an individual rebelling against the bureau, whether in the form of an office, the corporate world, or even the entire modern world. Moreover, perhaps with the exception of Tyler Durden, these characters are not portrayed as maladjusted, insane, or troublemakers. The bureaus are at fault. It is accepted in Office Space that corporate life is terrible and it is only because of the hypno therapy mis-hap that Peter has the wherewithal to walk away and not bother about the consequences. In the Matrix, the machines are literally sucking the life out of humankind and the Matrix is enabling them to do it. It is only because Neo discovers his ability to control the Matrix that he finds the courage to take on the machines and their agents and save humankind. The bureau is portrayed as a force that needs to be resisted and, if possible, destroyed.

While Americans remained hostile to the bureau circa the millennium, a look at these main characters shows that Americans may have begun to shake free of the radical individual. With the exception of Neo, none of these characters is particularly impressive. Peter doesn't have anything in particular he'd rather do than his programming job. In fact, he just wants to do nothing in particular. Similarly, the main character in Fight Club isn't anything to get excited about. He's a shallow chested, round shouldered man who spends his days terrorizing his boss and his nights fist-fighting other men in the city who have lost touch with their manhood. These characters just aren't extraordinary. What's important about them, though, is their ungovernability. Peter doesn't come into work and doesn't care when his boss confronts him about it. Tyler uses his insanity to scare his boss into leaving him alone. Neo can change the Matrix and is unable to be subdued by the machines' agents. These characters are ungovernable, if not very impressive, and we cheer them on because of it.

The television shows under consideration tend to focus less on a single character, but retain major characters. The show Archer is set in a spy agency in New York and follows a group of several secret agents, some support staff, and Sterling and Malory Archer, "the world's most dangerous spy" and his mother and spymaster, respectively. Community follows a motley study group at a second-rate community college called Greendale. Parks and Recreation follows the members of the parks department of the city government of Pawnee, a fictional town in Indiana.

Sterling Archer is the major character of the show Archer. Sterling is a self-centered, womanizing, vain, and likely alcoholic thirty-something man with an unhealthy relationship with his mother. Despite his moniker "the world's most dangerous spy," Sterling's performance in the field is frequently compromised by his inability to work with others. In one recurring plot device, Sterling gives away the position of himself and his partner/ex-lover because he's too busy fighting with her or accusing her of still being in love with him. Yet Sterling always manages to pull it off somehow. In one episode Sterling crashes the seaplane belonging to the man sent to find him after a three month disappearance. In the life boat, Sterling eats all the emergency rations and uses the flare gun to flag down a pirate ship that takes them captive. Nonetheless, by the end of the episode, Sterling has been made the pirate king. On the whole, there isn't much about Sterling that is likable. He has his charming moments, but they're fleeting. Still, it's hard not to like him.

It's less obvious that the show Community has a single major character. However, this examination will focus on Jeff Winger for purposes of analytic continuity. Jeff Winger is a thirty-something attorney who is attending classes at Greendale because he was disbarred when it was discovered his bachelor's degree is fake. Jeff is a self-centered womanizer and very vain. In one episode he gets kicked out of his PE class for refusing to change into his gym shorts because he doesn't "look cool in shorts." In another episode, Jeff encounters another attractive male who outperforms him in the pottery class Jeff is taking for an easy A. Jeff cannot cope with someone else being better than him and he has a breakdown. Though the study group regularly criticizes Jeff for being so self-centered and vain, they tend to look to him for guidance. In one episode, another character named Annie tells Jeff that he's "kind of like the dad of the group" and Jeff regularly uses his lawyerly oratorical and manipulation skills to resolve conflicts. Despite his negative character traits and initial emotional distance, Jeff comes to view the group as a sort of family. It's only when Jeff embraces his role within the group that he becomes likable.

Leslie Knope is the major character of the show Parks and Recreation. Leslie is the Deputy Director of the parks and recreation department. She is cheery and ambitious. Her role models include Hillary Clinton, Madeleine Albright, and Condoleezza Rice. One day Leslie hopes to be City Manager, but ultimately she would like to be President of the United States. Leslie's work is her identity. The walls of her office are lined with color-coded binders full of ideas she's had for the department. We learn through the course of the show that she doesn't seem ever to have had a successful romantic relationship. Nor does she seem to do any activities or have any friends that aren't work-related. In one episode, she hosts a dinner party in order to impress a potential love interest. We discover that Leslie can't cook a meal and hasn't unpacked her belongings despite the fact that she's lived in this house for years. Leslie hires the community class teachers, whose classes have recently been cut due to a budget crisis, to cook, clean, and entertain. Leslie is a bureaucrat, but we love her because she's smart, funny, and completely sincere in her enthusiasm for her work at the parks department.

There is a very different attitude toward the bureau on display in these television shows from what we saw in the films from 1999. There are no strong negative feelings towards the bureau in these shows. There are occasional labor-management conflicts in Archer, but the explanation is that Malory is being unreasonable. The same benign attitude toward the bureau is on display in Community. This show is set in a quintessential bureau—a school—yet the interactions we see between the study group and people in positions of authority are frequently friendly, though perhaps a little absurd. The professors tend to be unhinged and the dean, who has adopted the members of the study group as his favorites, periodically shows up in drag to give them news and hit on Jeff. In Parks and Recreation, the bureau is literally the characters' natural habitat. They are bureaucrats. Yet, here too we have an absurd portrayal of the bureau embodied by Leslie's boss—the bureaucrat who hates big government. In these shows, the bureau is portrayed as the harmless and humanized, though often absurd, background of the characters' lives.

There is also a very different and noticeable shift in attitude toward the radical individual in these shows. Of the major characters examined, Sterling Archer is the closest to the ungovernable radical individual, but it's evident the audience is supposed to recognize Sterling as an unlikable person. The same is true of Jeff Winger. He only becomes likable when he recognizes that he values the study group and accepts the responsibilities and expectations that imposes on him. Leslie Knope is by far the most likable of these characters, but she is also the furthest from the radical individual type. She is literally a bureaucrat. Further, none of these characters is truly ungovernable. Sterling may get out of hand on occasion, but his mother and co-workers keep him in line. Jeff realizes that he isn't special and his life is better with the study group. Each of these characters is fully integrated into the social groups of which they are part, often consciously so.

Comparison of the films from 1999 and the television shows from 2009 displays a significant cultural shift regarding the bureau and the radical individual. Carr's pop culture analysis signals growing dissonance between our political culture and the practical realities of life in the America of today. He warns that the stories we tell ourselves lead us to expect a life like Davy Crockett's or Rick Blaine's, but given the bureaucratic phenomenon, we find ourselves in the world of Dilbert. Indeed, this analysis bears out in 1999. Office Space, Fight Club, and the Matrix are stories of ungovernable individuals rebelling against and overthrowing the bureau. Carr warns that if we can't resolve this dissonance between our political culture and practical reality, Americans will go through life either deluded or disappointed.

However, when we turn to the television shows from 2009 we see a very different attitude toward the bureau and the individual. In Archer and Community, the major characters resembling the radical individual type are shamed and censored into getting along with others. Insofar as these characters resemble the ungovernable individual, they are portrayed as unlikable. In contrast, Leslie Knope is the perfect bureaucrat and she is exceedingly likable. Additionally, while each of these shows are set in a bureau, whether it be a spy agency, a community college, or a city government, the bureau is not seen as a threat. Moreover, the bureaucrats in these shows are portrayed as harmless, though often absurd, human beings. The bureau of 2009 has been defanged.

This is not to suggest that we have conclusively decided against radical individualism and in favor of the bureau. A fair amount of ambivalence is evident. Though Sterling and Jeff are portrayed as unlikable, we can't help but be drawn to them. This ambivalence is reflected in the other characters' attitudes towards them. Sterling's ex-lover repeatedly calls hims an "asshole" and yet it's clear she's still attracted to him. The other members of the study group may criticize Jeff's self-centeredness, vanity, and emotional distance, but their criticism often seems motivated by hurt feelings over Jeff's pronouncements that he doesn't need them.

This ambivalence is also evident in the continued appeal of movies such as the 2008 Iron Man, which has since become a franchise. Iron Man, or Tony Stark, is the quintessential ungovernable radical individual. It's interesting to note, though, that Tony Stark is independently wealthy, a genius, and battery-powered. While the success of the Iron Man franchise indicates that the radical individual still speaks to us, his highly unique circumstances seem a tacit nod to the unreality of this individual.

An update of the pop culture analysis suggests that we are making some progress on reconciling our political culture with the bureau. We see less vilification of the bureau and more impatience with the ungovernable individual. We've taken steps toward removing the dissonance between our political culture and the practical reality of life in America today. But ambivalence remains. This ambivalence is reflected in our pop culture and, indeed, in the 2012 presidential election. Both President Obama's and Governor Romney's visions of America continue to speak to us.

## CULTURE CRISIS

The foregoing pop culture analysis suggests our political culture has been evolving. We have been shaking ourselves free of our radical individualism and adopting the bureau as a necessary and even appealing feature of our lives. Davy Crockett and Randall Patrick McMurphy were until recently held up as heroes worthy of admiration and imitation. Today characters sharing their ungovernability are censored and portrayed as anti-heroes. The radical individual still fascinates us, but we are beginning to realize that the life of the radical individual will not be our life.

The shift between the films of 1999 and the films of 2009 show that we have begun to reevaluate our view of the bureau. Whereas the good life of the radical individual was incompatible with the bureau, we have begun to developed a revised picture of the good life. We have begun the process of adapting our picture of the good life to include the bureau. This is evident in the kinds of life decisions made by the members of Generation Y. Generation Y made life decisions with the demands of the bureau in mind. They went to college to obtain degrees and some knowledge that a bureau might find valuable. Many of them have worked unpaid or underpaid internships to gain experience in some industry. In order to fund these years of professional development, they took out massive school loans rationalizing this debt as an investment in their future.

The fundamental idea underlying these actions was the promise of the bureau. The members of Generation Y were taught that if they received a degree from a decent college or university and obtained some relevant work experience, they would find a career in a bureau. They were taught that if they played by the rules, kept their heads down, and did their work that they could expect to earn a living wage. Their lives might not be grand or glamorous, but they would be comfortable lives.

They could expect to have evenings, weekends, the occasional vacation, and some disposable income to live a comfortable, if modest, life.

The Recession has indelibly and irreversibly changed the lives of this generation of people. Young adults graduating from college following the 2008 Recession faced the worst job market in recent history. Burdened with thousands of dollars of loan debt, these recent graduates found themselves faced with a job market in which mid-salary jobs have been replaced with low-salary jobs. Unable to both support themselves and repay their student loans, many of these young adults moved back in with their parents, exchanging the name "Generation Y" for "the Boomerang Generation." Faced with uncertain financial futures, these young adults find themselves unable to attain the modest, but comfortable lives they've been told to expect. They are putting off buying houses, getting married, having children, and even simply buying a car.

The Recession has made our revised picture of the good life unattainable. This revised picture is a casualty of the 2008 Recession and its fall-out. The story the members of Generation Y told themselves about how their lives would go is no longer helpful in explaining their experience or guiding their life choices. This picture leads them to desire a kind of life that is no longer available. To continue to cling to it can only result in confusion and disappointment.

What this generation of Americans is facing is an instance of culture crisis. By "culture crisis" I mean a historical moment in which our culture comes apart from the practical realities of our lives.[25] In moments of culture crisis, our culture leads

---

[25]Readers familiar with Wittgenstein's thought may take issue with the distinction I am drawing here between "culture" and "practical reality" or "the world." After all, as we will see in the next chapter, Wittgenstein argues that we make the world through our language and culture. How, then, these readers will ask, could these things come apart? My response is two-fold. Firstly, I am only introducing the problem here. I will argue in the next chapter that we need a Wittgensteinian framework to make sense of the problem. To employ a Wittgensteinian framework here would be

us to expect a world drastically different from the one in which we find ourselves. In this case, the picture of the good life embedded in our political culture no longer helps us make sense of our lives. Generation Y is burdened with a pre-Recession picture of the good life in a post-Recession world.

The phenomenon of culture crisis is similar to cultural myth, such as the myth of the radical individual. These myths lead us to expect a world different from the world in which we find ourselves, as is the case in a moment of culture crisis. An individual in the grip of the myth of the radical individual, as Carr argues, expects to find himself in the world of Davy Crockett and Kit Carsen. This myth leads the individual to think he can make his own way, play by his own rules, and control his own destiny. The tragedy of such myths, as was discussed above, is that this individual does not live in the world of Davy Crockett and Kit Carsen, but in the world of Dilbert and Leslie Knope.

The phenomenon of culture crisis is similar to cultural myth, but it is also importantly different. In a moment of culture crisis, the expectation to find ourselves in a particular world is a reasonable expectation. The members of Generation Y expected to find themselves in the world of Dilbert and Leslie Knope. They expected to live the kind of life millions of people had been living until very recently. Whereas the life of the radical individual became a practical impossibility with the settlement of the frontier, the life of Dilbert and Leslie Knope became an impossibility almost over night a few years ago. The source of culture crisis is not a lack of sober assessment of the world in which one lives. Rather, the source of culture crisis is a sudden

---

fairly controversial and question-begging. Indeed, one of the questions of this thesis is how we even make sense of the phenomenon of culture crisis. Secondly, I think it is a mistake to think of culture as a self-consistent whole. I think it's fairly likely that our goals, values, and picture of the good life is always out of sync, to some degree, with technology and how we organize ourselves as a society. For the time being, I am employing this distinction in order to avoid begging the question. Later on I'll employ it for analytic clarity, though, of course, the Wittgensteinians won't like it.

and drastic change in the world in which one lives.

The members of Generation Y need a picture of the good life that can help them navigate life in a post-Recession world. Given that culture is a collective creation, this problem ultimately requires a collective solution. However, collective solutions take time and the individual has a life to live right now. Culture crisis can threaten to doom the individual to an unsatisfied and unfulfilled life simply because she was given a picture that doesn't match the world in which she finds herself. Such an individual is the topic of this thesis. The question that will be considered is: Is the individual caught in a moment of culture crisis fated to live an unfulfilled life or is there anything the individual can do to resolve the problem of culture crisis in her own case?

The liberal might find this question to be a non-starter. The liberal individual is, after-all, in control of her own destiny. This explanation, however, cannot account for the tenacity of the problem of culture crisis and is dismissive of culture itself. On the other hand, one might be inclined to say that as culture crisis is a community-wide problem, it needs a community-wide resolution. That seems right. Yet, the individual has a life to lead right now and she can't wait for everyone else to figure it out collectively.

The practical consequences of this problem should be clear. Nevertheless, the following investigation will be concerned with the conceptual underpinnings of culture crisis. This thesis will focus, in particular, on the philosophical thought of Wittgenstein and Nietzsche. I will argue in the next chapter that we need a Wittgensteinian view of language to make sense of the problem of culture crisis. I will argue in the third chapter that in order to avoid an unfulfilling life our individual needs to be something like a Nietzschean individual. The fourth chapter will argue that we need a Wittgensteinian view of language and culture to make sense of Nietzsche's idea of overcoming. The fifth chapter will consider whether Wittgenstein's view of language renders the Nietzschean individual a conceptual impossibility. The sixth chapter will assess the fate of our individual.

This chapter introduced the idea of political culture and traced the development of American political culture. Carr's bureaucratic phenomenon and his suggestion that it augurs a potentially fundamental change in political culture was explored. An extension of the analysis to the pop culture of today showed that we have made some progress in reconciling our political culture with the bureaucratic phenomenon. It was suggested that the growing recognition of the bureau as a benign feature of life was accompanied by the development of a revised picture of the good life in which the bureau was seen as a means to contentment and success. However, the fall-out of the 2008 Recession has rendered this developing picture of the good life unattainable and a source of disappointment.

Something is happening in America today. We can see it in the events that we read about in our newspapers and in the shows we watch during prime time. This culture crisis potentially means a whole generation of Americans are fated to live unsatisfying and unfulfilled lives. This thesis is concerned with these individuals. It asks whether these individuals are fated to pretend that the picture of the good life embedded in their pre-Recession political culture is adequate to the demands of their lives or whether they can free themselves from this picture and potentially find happiness.

# A WITTGENSTEINIAN WORLD

Wittgenstein's thought is not typically regarded as concerned with the human condition. Despite this tendency, there are numerous comments in his notebooks on such topics as religion, war, progress, and culture. These tend to be dismissed as casual observations. Wittgenstein is usually read as strictly concerned with the nature of language, mathematics, psychology, and philosophical method. Such topics are, it is assumed, obviously separate from the political, social, or cultural. Béla Szabados attributes this to the tendency in analytic philosophy to regard one's biographical and historical context as irrelevant to one's philosophical thought.[26]

Despite this tendency in Wittgenstein interpretation, several philosophers and theorists have seen a connection between Wittgenstein's thought and the human condition. This thesis represents another example. The aim of this chapter is to argue that we need something like a Wittgensteinian view of language in order to account for the phenomenon of culture crisis. First it will introduce the reader to the political and cultural side of Wittgenstein interpretation. Then it will argue that culture crisis is ultimately linguistic in nature because it is a conceptual failure. Several criteria will be enumerated that a view of language must meet if it is to account for culture crisis. It will be shown that a Wittgensteinian view of language can meet these criteria whereas a Russellian view cannot.

---

[26]Szabados (2010), 226. A similar but more cautious ground for ignoring these comments is to observe that Wittgenstein never elaborated a philosophy of the political or of culture. As such, anything we might say on the topic can only be speculation because we have no way of knowing what that was. This stance was articulated to me by Peter Hacker.

## CULTURE AND POLITICS IN WITTGENSTEIN

Despite the tendency in Wittgenstein interpretation to dismiss his comments on the
political, social, or cultural, several philosophers and theorists have seen a connection
between his thought and the human condition. First and foremost was Wittgenstein himself. Indeed, in an early draft of the foreward for *Philosophical Occasions*,
Wittgenstein wrote:

> This book is written for those who are in sympathy with the spirit in
> which it is written. This is not, I believe, the spirit of the main current of
> European and American civilization. The spirit of this civilization makes
> itself manifest in the industry, architecture and music of our time, in its
> fascism and socialism, and it is alien and uncongenial to the author.[27]

Further on in the draft he indicates that he thinks European and American civilization are marked by "the disappearance of a culture."[28] Such sentiments are reprised
in the preface to *Philosophical Investigations* in which he expresses doubt that the
book will be illuminating to its readers "in its poverty and in the darkness of this
time."[29] Thus, as von Wright has observed, though Wittgenstein did not give a
philosophy of the political or of culture he "thought that the problems with which
he was struggling were somehow connected with 'the way people live', that is, with
features of our culture or civilization. . . "[30]

Some philosophers and theorists have drawn theoretical implications from
Wittgenstein's view of language. Wittgenstein's idea that language is bound up
with what he called "forms of life" has led several social scientists to insist on greater
attention to language. Hanna Pitkin, for instance, uses Wittgenstein's work to argue

[27]Wittgenstein (1977), 6e.
[28]Wittgenstein (1977), 6e.
[29]Wittgenstein (1967), x.
[30]von Wright (1998), 110.

that in order to study action effectively, we first need to study the grammar of the word "action" to understand its nature.[31] Pitkin makes a similar argument about our political concepts like "justice."[32]

Hans Sluga extends this idea to political engagement by suggesting that active political engagement requires a working knowledge of our political concepts.[33] Wittgenstein's notion of family resemblance concepts, Sluga argues, suggests that our political concepts may have a multifaceted nature that differs from what we've assumed in the past.[34]

In a different vein, Peter Winch takes Wittgenstein's view of language to collapse the distinction between action and language.[35] In order to explain action, we must do what we do when we explain language: identify the rule that gives it meaning.[36] According to this view, the meaning of an individual's action is determined by the social rules or norms in which she partakes. David Bloor develops a similar reading to serve as the theoretical underpinnings of his sociological studies.[37]

Other interpreters have attempted to derive a specific political stance from Wittgenstein's views on language. János Nyíri, for example, argues that we should consider Wittgenstein as a conservative thinker. The core of Nyíri's argument is that because forms of life are the "given" in Wittgenstein's view, there is no perspective or ground from which to criticize them.[38] David Bloor further develops this conservative reading by arguing that if Edmund Burke had considered questions on the same level

---

[31]Pitkin (1972), 140-168, 241-262.
[32]Pitkin (1972), 182-191.
[33]Sluga (2011), 137.
[34]Sluga (2011), 138.
[35]Winch (1973), 121-128.
[36]Winch (1973), 50-63.
[37]Bloor (1983), Bloor (1997).
[38]Nyíri (1998), 58-59.

of abstraction as Wittgenstein, he would have come up with very similar answers.[39]

Others have found the conservative reading to rest upon a limited or mistaken understanding of Wittgenstein's view. David Cerbone, for instance, argues that conservative readings take concepts and forms of life to be more separable than Wittgenstein intended.[40] Pitkin argues that some of our concepts, like "justice," contain standards of judgment which allow us to critique current practices or institutions.[41]

More recently, Christopher Robinson has suggested that Wittgenstein was simply dissatisfied with scientism and the rise of the bureaucracy rather than with modernity as a whole.[42] On Robinson's account, Wittgenstein gave his view of language as a way of reversing the damage done to trust by war, genocide, and terrorism, as well as providing a means of resisting the bureaucratization of society.[43]

The work of these theorists and philosophers is invaluable. However, Wittgenstein's comments regarding his own work suggest that he sees a much more intimate connection between his view of language and the human condition. There is evidence of this as early as the *Tractatus Logico-Philosophicus*. In a letter to his publisher, Wittgenstein insisted that "the point of the book [the *Tracatus*] was ethical."[44]

Despite Wittgenstein's insistence, interpreters have had difficulty making sense of this remark. For instance, unable to understand Wittgenstein's claim that the ethical is unsayable, Daniel McManus invokes the idea of the inner voice of God or conscience to explain what Wittgenstein must mean.[45] Cora Diamond suggests

---

[39]Bloor (2004), 113.
[40]Cerbone (2003), Cf. Crary (2000).
[41]Pitkin (1972), 182-217.
[42]Robinson (2009), 89-90.
[43]Robinson (2009), 61, 98. Robinson's argument is fairly opaque and relies heavily on a metaphor of walking as well as speculation on how Wittgenstein must have felt during the war.
[44]Quoted in Monk (1990), 178.
[45]McManus (2006), 175-176, 181-182.

that we read these ethical propositions in the same way as metaphysical non-sense propositions: imaginatively, using our imagination to understand what the non-sense propositions are trying to tell us.[46] In the case of metaphysical non-sense propositions, this imaginative engagement is thought to be therapeutic, ridding us of the temptation to such propositions.[47] Assuming this is a good reading of the *Tractatus*,[48] it still does not help us understand its ethical dimension as Diamond insists the ethical propositions are not meant to be therapeutic in the same way. Peter Hacker takes an alternate approach and simply dismisses the ethical comments as tacked on and poorly integrated into the rest of the work.[49]

Fortunately, we needn't speculate. Wittgenstein elaborated on the ethical aspect of the *Tractatus* eight years after its publication in his "A Lecture on Ethics." He uses the term "ethics" broadly to mean "the enquiry into what is valuable... the meaning of life, or into what makes life worth living, or into the right way of living."[50] He clarifies that he is interested only in instrinsic or absolute values, as opposed to relative or trivial values. By relative values, he means values relative to a standard or purpose. Thus, if I say "This is a good knife" the goodness here is relative to the standard of chopping or slicing efficiently. That is, it's a good knife because of the fact that it is sharp. The difference between relative and absolute values, he claims, is that relative values are statements of fact whereas "no statement of fact can ever be, or imply, a judgment of absolute value."[51] No proposition can imply a judgment of absolute value because propositions only assert facts. The whole set

---

[46]Diamond (2000), 156-158.
[47]Diamond (2000), 160.
[48]There is reason to think it's not. Cf. Hacker (2003).
[49]From conversation. Hacker speculates that Wittgenstein's concern with the ethical here is a manifestation of post-traumatic stress disorder from serving in the war.
[50]Wittgenstein (1965), 5.
[51]Wittgenstein (1965), 6.

of true propositions, he says, is just the whole of natural science and there are no propositions of value among them.[52] This is the view of language he set out in the *Tractatus*.[53] As absolute value is not part of the natural world, he refers to it as the "supernatural."[54]

Putative ethical propositions are non-sense, then, because they do not assert facts. Insofar as our ethical propositions do have sense, Wittgenstein argues, they do not have the sense we want. They are essentially non-sense.[55] This is consistent with his claim in the *Tractatus* that "ethics cannot be put into words."[56] However, the fact that we cannot talk about ethics does not mean that we should neglect it. Indeed, Wittgenstein closes the lecture by emphasizing the importance of ethics. Ethics, he says, "so far as it springs from the desire to say something about the ultimate meaning of life, the absolute good, the absolute valuable, can be no science... But it is a document of a tendency in the human mind which I personally cannot help respecting deeply..."[57] Though we may not be able to speak of it sensibly, ethics is a significant concern.

In the preface to the *Tractatus*, Wittgenstein says of his work:

> I therefore believe myself to have found, on all essential points, the final solution of the problems. And if I am not mistaken in this belief, then the second thing in which the value of this work consists is that it shows how little is achieved when these problems are solved.[58]

The problems to which he is referring are the problems of clarifying the relationship between language and the world. Wittgenstein claims he has solved these problems.

---

[52]Wittgenstein (1965), 6-7.
[53]Cf. Wittgenstein (1961), 3.203, 4.022, 4.1, 4.5, 6.42.
[54]Wittgenstein (1961), 6.41.
[55]Wittgenstein (1965), 11.
[56]Wittgenstein (1961), 6.421.
[57]Wittgenstein (1965), 12.
[58]Wittgenstein (1961), 4.

But this view assumes language is essentially an instrument of science. Wittgenstein's claim that he has shown how little is achieved when we have solved these problems suggests that science cannot discover or explain the meaning of life for us. We must address these most important questions in some other way. This is the sentiment he expresses at the end of the *Tractatus* when he says, "We feel that even when all *possible* scientific questions have been answered, the problems of life remain completely untouched. Of course, there are then no questions left, and this itself is the answer."[59] We have to look for what makes life valuable somewhere else and in some other way.[60]

The aim of exploring the ethical in Wittgenstein's early thought was to get some sense as to what Wittgenstein saw as the connection between language and the human condition. The suggestion is that it follows from Wittgenstein's early view of language that value and the meaning of life are outside the jurisdiction of science. Wittgenstein later gives up this view of language, but this does not mean he gave up interest in what makes life valuable. Indeed, there is likely a connection here with the comments Wittgenstein made a year later regarding the disappearance of culture in his draft foreword for the *Philosophical Occasions* and his darkness comment in the preface for *Philosophical Investigations*. For now, however, let's turn to the relationship between culture crisis and language.

---

[59]Wittgenstein (1961), 6.52.
[60]Cf. Sluga (2011), 41-55, Pears (1985), 57, 88, Pitkin (1972), 30.

## CULTURE CRISIS AND LANGUAGE

The previous section considered the connection Wittgenstein and others have seen between his work and the human condition. This section will consider the relationship between culture crisis and language. As we saw in the first chapter, "political culture" refers to the shared norms and beliefs that make a group of people into a political unit. It consists of the basic assumptions and values that we employ in our everyday lives.

In times of culture crisis some aspect of our culture leads us to expect a world drastically different from the one we find ourselves in. In the case of Generation Y the idea of the good life embedded in the political culture is no longer attainable. This idea leads the individual members of Generation Y to expect their lives to go a certain way. However, this pre-Recession idea of the good life can only be a source of frustration and dissatisfaction in a post-Recession world.

We can make sense of the phenomenon of culture crisis as a failure of concepts. Concepts, like the basic assumptions and values of political culture, tell us how things are and how we should proceed. Liberal political culture, for instance, tells us that individuals are capable of setting their own goals and determining the course of their own lives and that they should be treated that way. In terms of concepts, what this means is that in liberal political culture, the concept "person" means an individual capable of setting her own goals and determining the course of her own life. It is also part of the concept "person" that such an individual should be treated as an individual capable of setting their own goals and determining the course of their own life. We can, then, think of political culture as a shared set of interrelated concepts. On this conceptual understanding of political culture, then, culture crisis occurs when our concepts no longer fit the world in which we find ourselves.

The philosophy of language is the study of the nature of concepts, words, propositions, thought, and the relationships between them. Since culture crisis is a conceptual failure, an adequate view of language should be able to account for this phenomenon. Due to the complex nature of culture crisis, it may be helpful to enumerate criteria that a view of language must fulfill if it is to account for culture crisis. These criteria simply capture aspects of political culture and culture crisis as described in the first chapter. They are are: 1) account for the fact that concepts can have both normative and descriptive aspects; 2) account for the fact that concepts change; 3) account for the dissonance between our concepts and the world; 4) account for the collective nature of culture crisis; and 5) account for the tenacity of the problem of culture crisis. To show that these criteria do exclude at least some views we will consider whether Bertrand Russell's view of language can meet them.[61]

The initial thought underlying Russell's view of language is highly intuitive. The purpose of language, he assumes, is to describe the world. This is a simple beginning. On Russell's view, a proposition is a complex of words. These words are like names that stand for various kinds of objects. They might stand for a person, an object, a relation, or a property. A proposition is true so long as the relation asserted to hold among the constituents of the proposition obtains in the world. Thus, the proposition "The book is blue" is true because the book I'm referring to stands in the predication relation to the color blue. So far this seems unproblematic.

Russell's view gets more complicated from here. He philosophized in the hey-day of sense-data. The idea behind sense-data is that the knowledge I have of

---

[61]Russell's view of language is similar in substance and motivation to views forwarded by other thinkers, such as Plato and Kant. The focus on Russell is meant to simplify the discussion for the reader as well as to remain true to Wittgenstein's biography. The reader should keep in mind, however, that Russell's view is examined as an example of a class of views on the nature of language.

the world depends upon my experience of the world through my sense perceptors. Strictly speaking, then, I don't see a blue book. Rather, I see a rectangular-shaped blue patch in my visual field. This sense-data idea leads Russell to conclude that what I really know when I assert the true proposition "The book is blue" is not directly anything about the book, but rather something about my sense-data.

However, Russell wasn't a sceptic about the external world. Indeed, he firmly believed that there are physical objects. He just thought we didn't have any direct knowledge about them. In his terminology, we don't have knowledge of physical objects by acquaintance, as we do our sense-data.[62] We only know physical objects by description.[63] That is, I know that there is an object that must satisfy the description "The object causing a rectangular-shaped blue patch in my visual field right now." In fact, Russell thinks that most words are really shorthand for such sense-data descriptions.[64] Thus, when I assert the seemingly simple and unproblematic sentence "The book is blue" what I am actually asserting is a very long proposition about sense-data. What makes it true is that there is such an object (a book) and it actually does stand in the predication relation to the color blue.

It's here that Russell's view of language gets really interesting. Despite the fact that we think we're talking about physical objects and we intend to make assertions about physical objects, we really only ever manage to make assertions about sense-data.[65] Nonetheless, Russell maintains that when I say "The book is blue" and when you say "The book is blue," we're both talking about the same blue book.[66]

---

[62]Russell (1910-1911), 109-112. For the sake of completeness, Russell also believed that we have knowledge of ourselves, concepts (as opposed to particulars), and universal relations, but this isn't directly relevant to the discussion here.
[63]Russell (1910-1911), 112-113.
[64]Russell (1910-1911), 114.
[65]Russell (1910-1911), 116, 117, 127.
[66]Russell (1910-1911), 116.

That blue book, after all, is what makes our respective assertions true. But, because the sense-data I have are different from the sense-data you have, the propositions we assert are different. The proposition in my mouth consists of different descriptions than the proposition in your mouth.[67] Despite this difference, Russell maintains that what matters for communication is just that the same objects answer to our different descriptions.[68]

Though Russell's view of language started from a highly intuitive idea, the resulting account his highly unintuitive. The seemingly simple sentence "The book is blue," once subjected to a Russellian analysis is hardly simple at all. Indeed, this superficial simplicity is only a shorthand for a very long proposition about sense-data. On Russell's view we only ever manage to speak and think about physical objects indirectly. Moreover, while two people may assert the same set of true propositions, these propositions necessarily have different analyses and different meanings for these two people. Russell's analysis maintains our initial intuition that language describes the world at the price of a highly unintuitive explanation of meaning and thought.

It's not clear that Russell's view of language can even begin to account for culture crisis. This is so even if we ignore Russell's thoroughly thin view of concepts according to which concepts are simply general terms like "triangle," "leaf," and "red." With regard to criterion 1), Russell's view of language draws a strict dividing line between the descriptive and the normative. With regards to criterion 2), since words are taken to be names or descriptions for people, objects, relations, or properties and these are constituents of the world, it's not clear that there's any room for these to change. With regards to criterion 3), insofar as we could make sense of this criterion, it seems as though a Russellian would have to say that we'd simply gotten

---

[67]Russell (1910-1911), 114-115.
[68]Russell (1910-1911), 116.

things wrong. Language represents the world. If it doesn't, it's because we've made a mistake. As for criteria 4) and 5) the only account that appears available to the Russellian is to claim that we have all made the same mistake and continue to fail to see our error.

The initial thought underlying Russell's view of language is intuitive. However, the resultant view is highly unintuitive and it is unable to clearly account for any aspect of culture crisis. This in no way constitutes a conclusive argument against views of language that start from a similar initial thought, but it should serve to raise suspicion.[69] If we accept the conceptual rendering of culture crisis, then any adequate view of language should be able to account for this phenomenon. The Russellian view can't even begin to meet this standard.

## WITTGENSTEIN ON LANGUAGE

Wittgenstein, too, was initially impressed by the Russellian view of language. Indeed, in the *Tractatus* he offers a view of language which is largely a refinement of Russell's. By the early 1930's, however, Wittgenstein seriously began to question the Russellian view of language. Having spent the early part of his philosophical career in the thrall of such a view, he understood its seemingly irresistible obviousness. Indeed, similar views on the nature of language continue to enjoy wide-spread adherence and advocacy today.

In the *Philosophical Investigations*, Wittgenstein presents a concerted attack on views like Russell's. As was seen in the previous section, such views start with what seem to be obvious and intuitively true insights. The purpose of language, Russell thought, was to describe the world via true propositions. This view takes the

---

[69]Cf. Sluga (2011), 74.

description of the world or the production of true propositions to be the essential function of language. By the time he was working on the *Philosophical Investigations*, Wittgenstein rejects this view and the argument from intuition on which it relies. Intuition is neither an argument for a philosophical position nor an insight into the nature of things.[70]

Wittgenstein further criticizes the Russellian view, and his own view in the *Tractatus*, for imposing requirements upon the nature of language. That is, the Russellian view assumes that language has a simple, uniform, logically consistent nature. Wittgenstein argues, however, that the "more narrowly we examine actual language, the sharper becomes the conflict between it" and this requirement.[71] Despite this conflict, Russell and others fail to consider that language does not have a simple, uniform, logically consistent structure.

Wittgenstein brings out the inadequacy of such a view of language with an example of a primitive language. This language is used by two builders. The language consists of the words "block," "pillar," "slab," and "beam." When one builder calls out one of these words, the other brings the appropriate kind of stone. This is an example of a language wherein words are like names, as in Russell's view, but it hardly approximates the complexity of our language.[72]

Views such as Russell's find their motivation in the conviction that getting clear on the nature of language will help us solve other philosophical problems. The assumption is that because the language we use only approximates language in its pure, formal, logically consistent form, we get confused. Our questions have answers. The solution will become clear once we clean up our language. In contrast,

---

[70]Wittgenstein (1967), §254, §299.

[71]Wittgenstein (1967), §107.

[72]Wittgenstein (1967), §2, Cf. Wittgenstein (1967), §107, §114.

Wittgenstein complains in the *Philosophical Investigations* that this gets the nature of language wrong. This view assumes that language is transcendent or supernatural. Instead, Wittgenstein argues that the concept "language" is just like other mundane concepts: messy, complicated, and an organic human creation.[73]

Wittgenstein realized that the initial obviousness of views such as Russell's was due to the questions we were asking. The suggestion is that the initial intuitiveness of a Russellian view of language is the result of asking after the meanings of words. The temptation is to take a simple and supposedly representative sentence such as "The book is blue" and look for a referent for each of the words.[74] This tends to lead to views like Russell's.

Wittgenstein begins his *Philosophical Investigations* by suggesting that we change the questions we ask about language. Rather than asking after the meanings of words, Wittgenstein admonishes us to ask how we use words.[75] This question brings to our attention the various, if related, ways in which we use a particular word and the multitude of things we do with language.[76] It also allows us to recognize the role tone and facial expression play in language.[77] The focus on how we use words allows us to see the messy, complicated, and organic nature of language.

Wittgenstein introduces the term "language-game" to capture this new understanding of language. The invocation of the notion of games is meant to emphasize that language is an activity in which we engage.[78] Giving orders, reporting an event,

---

[73]Wittgenstein (1967), §97, §108.
[74]Wittgenstein (1958), 1.
[75]Wittgenstein (1958), §1, §4, §43, §§73-74, Wittgenstein (1967), §1, §20.
[76]Wittgenstein (1967), §23, §27, §§65-67, Cf. Wittgenstein (1958), §§17-20, §§137-139, §xi.
[77]Wittgenstein (1967), §21.
[78]Wittgenstein (1967), §23.

forming a hypothesis, making up a story, guessing riddles, asking, cursing, and praying are examples of some activities we can only do by means of language.[79] But Wittgenstein sees the relationship between language and our activities as more fundamental than these examples indicate. Language, he insists, is "part of an activity, or a form of life" where form of life refers to the institutions, practices or customs of a community.[80] Elsewhere Wittgenstein equates language with a culture.[81]

Through its concepts, our language both reflects and enables us to engage in our form of life. For instance, the concept of marriage both reflects that we are a society that engages in legally and religiously sanctioned unions between two people and enables us to engage in this practice. Our concepts depend upon our form of life for their meaning. As our form of life changes, so too do our concepts.[82]

The language-game understanding of language is also meant to bring to our attention that language is governed by rules. Games are only games if there are rules which determine correct gameplay. In the case of language, the rules governing a word tell us what kind of thing its referent is as well as the ways and contexts in which we can use the word. Just as the rules which govern correct gameplay, the rules which determine correct usage of words are conventions. They are conventions we have created and accepted as guiding our moves within the language-game.

The rules governing the use of a word take certain normal conditions for granted. For instance, just as the rules of checkers do not tell the players what to do in case a passing seagull eats half the pieces, the rules governing the meaning of "measure" do not tell us what to do in case objects start changing size.[83] The rules,

[79]Wittgenstein (1967), §23.
[80]Wittgenstein (1967), §23, §199.
[81]Wittgenstein (1958), 134-135.
[82]Wittgenstein (1967), §18, §19, §23.
[83]Wittgenstein (1967), §142.

then, are indefinite. However, the fact that the meaning of a word is determined by an indefinite rule does not mean the meaning of the word is indefinite. The words operate perfectly well within normal conditions.[84] We know, generally, how to use them.[85] Language is an activity governed by indefinite rules.[86]

In addition to the messiness of indefinite rules, Wittgenstein's language-game view takes language to be inherently complicated. Whereas Russell believes that in proper, formalized language words have one definite meaning, Wittgenstein eschews this stance. Indeed, Wittgenstein further distances himself from a Russellian view by introducing the idea of "family resemblance" concepts. The idea of a family resemblance concept is that for some concepts there is no common feature or unifying essence that is shared by all the items to which the concept applies.[87]

Wittgenstein famously uses the example of games to illustrate this point. There is no single set of characteristics common to all games. Some involve balls, some cards, some are played with others and some played only with oneself.[88] Many of our concepts, Wittgenstein argues, are unbounded like this. Nonetheless, there is, he says, a family resemblance among the various things we call games. Though they may not all have some characteristic in common, the different kinds of games are "related" to each other in various ways.[89]

Though language is messy and complicated, Wittgenstein is not sceptical about getting clear on the meanings of our words. We can achieve this by engaging in investigation of what he refers to as its "grammar." The grammar of a word consists of the rules governing its use and the family resemblance relations that might obtain

---

[84]Wittgenstein (1967), SS81-88.
[85]Wittgenstein (1967), SS148-155.
[86]Cf. Wittgenstein (1977), 78e, Wittgenstein (1958) §25, §43.
[87]Wittgenstein (1967), §67.
[88]Wittgenstein (1967), §66.
[89]Wittgenstein (1967), §65.

between different uses. By investigating the grammar of a particular word, we can get clear on the nature of the related concept.[90] For instance, in the appropriate circumstances the sentence "This color is red" is a grammatical statement which tells us that "red" is a color word and, when accompanied by an appropriate sample, this statement tells us which color it is. In investigating the concept "red," we might come across the phrases "He saw red" and "Her cheeks flushed red" and note that in some cases red has to do with anger and embarrassment or, perhaps, arousal.

On Wittgenstein's language-game view of language, our relationship to language is profound. Language is not merely a means of describing the world or communicating thoughts. Rather, a language, a form of life—a culture—comes with its own world-picture.[91] When we learn language we don't only learn a bunch of words, or even how to do certain things with words. Rather, we learn a total system of concepts and judgments.[92] When we learn language we become enculturated into a total way of seeing and understanding the world. This can include everything from empirical judgments to religious beliefs.[93] The concepts of our language tell us how the world is, what kind of thing we are, and what kind of life is worth living. This world-picture is the implicit background of our activities and the lives we lead.[94] The world is as our world-picture tells us it is.

On a Wittgensteinian view of language, then, language is a system of concepts. We impose an order on the world via our concepts. They constitute our world-picture and, as such, are closely bound up with our form of life and our activities. In learning language we are taught to see and understand the world in a particular way. We

---

[90]Wittgenstein (1967), §371, §373.
[91]Wittgenstein (1969), §162, §211.
[92]Wittgenstein (1969), §105, §140, §141, §144.
[93]Wittgenstein (1969), §32, §53, §60, §85, §298.
[94]Wittgenstein (1969), §144, §472, §476.

accept certain judgments about how the world is and how we should live and act without question. We are initiated into a particular culture. We learn to see and act in accordance with the messy, complicated, organic human creation of language.

Wittgenstein was particularly fascinated with the phenomenon of entanglement. The rules of our language, typically, guide us without trouble. However, there are times when we become entangled in the rules of our language. Wittgenstein notes that this happens, for instance, in mathematics:

> The fundamental fact here is that we lay down rules, a technique, for a game, and that when we follow the rules, things do not turn out as we had assumed. That we are therefore as it were entangled in our own rules.
> This entanglement in our rules is what we want to understand (i.e. get a clear view of).[95]

In moments of entanglement, we become trapped within our concepts, unable to see our way out. This, for instance, is what Wittgenstein thinks has happened with philosophers investigating the nature of language. Philosophers have been unable to get clear on the nature of language, Wittgenstein suggests, because they are trapped within their concept of what language is and how it operates.[96]

Wittgenstein takes the aim of philosophy to be freeing ourselves from such entanglements. He, admittedly, holds a very conservative view of the nature of philosophy. Philosophy does not free us from these entanglements by altering our concepts. Philosophy leaves things as they are.[97] However, philosophy's investigation into the rules of our concepts and the underlying language-game view of language provides us a means of escape from entanglement. Such investigations show us that

---

[95]Wittgenstein (1967), §125.
[96]Wittgenstein (1967), §§89-108.
[97]Wittgenstein (1967), §124.

the problem lies in our concepts which are human creations and, therefore, capable of human re-creation.[98]

Now that we have a basic understanding of Wittgenstein's view of language, let's consider whether it can account for culture crisis. Criterion 1) requires an account for the fact that concepts can have both descriptive and normative aspects. Wittgenstein's view can easily meet this criterion. The concepts of our world-picture both describe how the world is and how we should proceed. Criterion 2) requires an account of conceptual change. On Wittgenstein's view because our concepts are shaped by our form of life, changes in this compel changes in our concepts. Criterion 3) requires an account of dissonance between our concepts and the practical realities of our lives. This would occur on Wittgenstein's view if conditions strayed beyond the boundaries of normal conditions. In such a situation, our concepts lead us to expect one world, but we find ourselves in another. We are entangled. Wittgenstein's view meets criterion 4) by the fact that our world-picture is shared by the other members of our language community.

The interesting aspect of the Wittgensteinian view of language is its response to criterion 5). This criterion requires that a view of language account for the tenacity of the problem of culture crisis. Wittgenstein's view meets this criterion by pointing to the mundanity of our world-picture. As Wittgenstein observes in a 1947 comment, this world-picture "lies in front of everyone's eyes."[99] This picture is so fundamental to our every experience, our testing and confirming of hypotheses, our making judgments, and our activities that often we don't even realize it is there to question it. The problem of culture crisis is tenacious because we often don't know to look for the problem in the right place.

---

[98]Wittgenstein (1967), §109, §§114-115, §129, cf. §374, §401.
[99]Wittgenstein (1977), 63, Cf. Wittgenstein (1977), 39.

The problem of culture crisis can be rephrased in Wittgensteinian terms as: A historical moment when our world-picture ceases to be a good one. In the case of Generation Y, this problem arises because the picture of the good life they were given leads them to expect and desire a kind of life that is no longer available. However, due to the suddenness of the transition to a post-Recession world and the mundanity of our world-picture, Generation Y continues to operate with a pre-Recession world-picture. In order to resolve this problem, Generation Y needs to adopt a world-picture better suited to the post-Recession world. The question is whether this is a solution available to the individual by herself.

This chapter opened with a consideration of the connection between Wittgenstein's thought and the human condition. Many philosophers and theorists have seen a connection, including Wittgenstein himself. An examination of the ethical in the *Tractatus* suggested that it follows from Wittgenstein's early view of language that science cannot tell us what makes life valuable. Wittgenstein tells us to look elsewhere for meaning. This advice rests on the strict division between fact and value assumed in Wittgenstein's early thought. But this division is absent from his later thought. Our whole world-picture—fact, value, and everything else—is the shadow of the concepts of our language. This view of language can help us make sense of the phenomenon of culture crisis in a way a Russellian view of language cannot.

Yet, it remains unclear if there is anything the individual can do to resolve the problem of culture crisis in her own case. Chapter five will consider the suggestion that appeal to a Wittgensteinian view of language renders the individual unable to do anything about the problem of culture crisis. This suggestion rests upon collectivist or communitarian readings of Wittgenstein's view on language, according to which language is essentially social. In the meantime, the next chapter will introduce the Nietzschean individual. It will be suggested that if the individual is to solve the problem of culture crisis in her own case, she must be something like the Nietzschean individual.

# THE NIETZSCHEAN INDIVIDUAL

Nietzsche is a highly controversial figure in the history of philosophy. In contrast to Wittgenstein, the connection between Nietzsche's thought and the human condition is impossible to deny. More difficult is identifying something palatable and coherent in his thought. After his works were appropriated for Nazi propaganda, some commentators argued that his focus is the moral and individual, not the political. More recently, philosophers and theorists have tried to extract from Nietzsche a theory of the political centered around the noble individual. Perhaps due to his blustering style and his uncompromising elitism, Nietzsche's thought tends to be received as somewhat sinister. Indeed, in a 2004 preface to his work *Nietzsche as Philosopher*, Arthur Danto points to a high school massacre in Pearl River, Mississippi as evidence that Nietzsche's writings need to be deflated and demythologized.[100]

While the connection to the human condition in Nietzsche's work is uncontroversial, there is little consensus as to what the connection is. After a survey of some of the literature, it will be suggested that the answer remains unclear because Nietzsche interpretation tends to focus on one aspect of his thought and neglect the others. An alternate interpretation will be presented according to which Nietzsche is a culture critic who examined politics, religion and morality, philosophy, and science as symptoms of the state of culture in late nineteenth century Europe. The aim of this chapter will be to isolate Nietzsche's new philosopher, that diasporic class of

---

[100]Danto (2005), xiii.

individuals Nietzsche hoped would carry out a cultural revival. I will refer to the new philosopher as the "Nietzschean individual."

## THE INDIVIDUAL AND THE POLITICAL IN NIETZSCHE

In his *Nietzsche: Philosopher, Psychologist, Anti-Christ*, published in 1950, Walter Kaufmann offered one of the first comprehensive, post-World War II studies of Nietzsche's thought. One of his over-arching aims in this work was to domesticate Nietzsche and distance him from the Nazis. To this end, Kaufmann argued that Nietzsche was concerned with the individual rather than the political.[101] Kaufmann admits that Nietzsche was critical of the state, but, he counters, this criticism is due to the fact that the state encourages mediocrity and is, thereby, inimical to the individual.[102] Other political comments, Kaufmann explains, are simply analogies about the individual.[103]

Kaufmann's project of domesticating Nietzsche extends beyond denying any direct interest in the political. Indeed, Kaufmann also denies that Nietzsche is interested in undermining or, to use a Nietzschean term, engaging in a revaluation of our Christian moral values. Instead of engaging in a critique of our values, Kaufmann argues that Nietzsche's revaluation is an internal criticism of our morality. Nietzsche employs our values to show that our standards are "poisonously immoral."[104] Despite appearances, then, Nietzsche is not interested in undermining or questioning our values. Such a project, Kaufmann insists, would only serve to exacerbate the real problem.

---

[101]Kaufmann (1950), 137, 210, 249, 357, 359.
[102]Kaufmann (1950), 103, 138-140, 357.
[103]Kaufmann (1950), 168-170, 174.
[104]Kaufmann (1950), 90-95.

Rather than the political or Christian morality, Kaufmann maintains that Nietzsche's major focus is nihilism.[105] Kaufmann glosses nihilism as a condition resulting from the realization that our values are worthless and, thereby, fail to give our lives meaning.[106] Unless it can be avoided, nihilism threatens to result in chaos, social disorder, and "universal madness."[107] According to Kaufmann, Nietzsche identifies the combination of Christianity and Darwinism as the source of nihilism in nineteenth century Europe. Christianity, he explains, locates value in God and the supernatural. Darwinism, on the other hand, denies God and thus denies value altogether.[108] Nihilism is the result of the realization that we are animals and cannot even look to the supernatural for meaning or salvation from our beastly state.

The unifying project of Nietzsche's work, Kaufmann tells us, is to battle this crisis of values. The problem is to restore the dignity of humankind while acknowledging our animalic nature.[109] Nietzsche, says Kaufmann, looks to the will to power, self-overcoming, and the Übermensch to resolve the problem of nihilism. The individual engages in self-overcoming, cultivating her nature so as to become more rational, more like the Übermensch.[110] The process of self-overcoming, on Kaufmann's picture, is a manifestation of the will to power. In self-overcoming one's reason exerts power on the chaos of one's passions and impulses, giving them order.[111] Through progressive application of reason to the passions, one becomes more powerful, rational, and human.[112] The individual comes more and more to resemble the Übermensch, a powerful and throughly rational individual who lives

---

[105]Kaufmann (1950), 102.
[106]Kaufmann (1950), 103.
[107]Kaufmann (1950), 80-85, 142.
[108]Kaufmann (1950), 86.
[109]Kaufmann (1950), 137.
[110]Kaufmann (1950), 150, 160, 166.
[111]Kaufmann (1950), 193, 199, 204.
[112]Kaufmann (1950), 213.

according to his own moral code.[113]

The Nietzsche with which Kaufmann presents us is a moral perfectionist. On this picture, the moral individual is that person who strives to become an Übermensch by employing reason to order and control her passions and impulses. Kaufmann introduces this reason-passion distinction to resolve a conceptual problem related to self-overcoming. Namely, he needs two things: One to overcome the other. While this understanding of self-overcoming is convenient, it fails to take account of Nietzsche's thoroughly post-Enlightenment view of the self. Admittedly, Kaufmann recognizes that Nietzsche rejects mind-body dualism.[114] Nonetheless, Kaufmann relies on dualism in his understanding of overcoming and we see it again in his explanation of guilt.[115] Without dualism, then, Kaufmann is unable to give a coherent explanation of self-overcoming.

Arthur Danto attempts to deflate and demythologize Nietzsche in his *Nietzsche as Philosopher* by capitalizing on the difficulty of making coherent the idea of self-overcoming. Danto understands nihilism to be an outgrowth of Nietzsche's perspectivist theory of truth. According to this perspectivism, all our beliefs and judgments are, strictly speaking, false.[116] There is no possible metaphysical or supernatural foundation for our beliefs and judgments.[117] Rather, our beliefs and judgments are simply the implications of a system of concepts that we have laid on

[113]Kaufmann (1950), 217-218, 267-272.

[114]Kaufmann (1950), 225-231.

[115]Kaufmann (1950), 220.

[116]Danto (2005), 15.

[117]Danto (2005), 17. The astute reader may note that the premise that our beliefs and judgments are false does not follow trivially from the premise that our beliefs have no supernatural or metaphysical foundation. Rather there is no basis for truth or falsity in this case. This is, however, the view Danto attributes to Nietzsche. In the next chapter, I will examine Clark's reading of Nietzsche. Clark, a student of Danto, argues that Nietzsche assumes a metaphysical correspondence theory of truth according to which a belief is true if and only if it has a foundation in the metaphysical or supernatural. I argue in the next chapter that this is a misreading of Nietzsche. It seems, however, that this assumption belongs to Danto.

the world, but we cannot get to anything in the world that makes this system correct or its truths true.[118] Danto takes Nietzsche's work to be directed at bringing the empty conventionality of our beliefs and judgments to our attention.[119] The problem of nihilism, on Danto's gloss, is the problem of how we manage to endure our lives once we accept this fact.[120]

Danto hopes to undermine what he takes to be the more harmful aspects of Nietzsche's thought. Specifically, he tries to show that Nietzsche's attempt to unleash the amoral and "antisocial passions" of the individual rests upon an inconsistency.[121] Danto claims that Nietzsche's rejection of metaphysics commits him to defending common sense.[122] Common sense comes with its own standard of truth, which Danto identifies as the "metaphysics of the herd."[123] The Nietzschean individual, being an antisocial non-conformist, is supposed to reject the beliefs and standards of common sense. However, Danto argues, the individual cannot get outside the perspective he's been socialized into in order to critique it.[124] He cannot overcome. In Danto's words "we remain forever imprisioned within ramified structures which, like spiders, we have produced ourselves..."[125] Though Nietzsche's perspectivism motivated his encouraging the individual to overcome, this same perspectivism makes this impossible. Without the Nietzschean individual, Danto argues, Nietzsche's work serves to show how thoroughly socialized we are.[126]

---

[118]Danto (2005), 12, 14-15, 49.
[119]Danto (2005), 80.
[120]Danto (2005), 17, 50.
[121]Danto (2005), 127.
[122]Danto (2005), 57.
[123]Danto (2005), 59.
[124]Danto (2005), 60. This criticism is, of course, reminiscent of the conservative reading of Wittgenstein. Indeed, Danto explicitly refers to Wittgenstein in building up this criticism of Nietzsche. Danto (2005), 104.
[125]Danto (2005), 82-83.
[126]Danto (2005), 105, 119, 121, 126.

More recently there has been a revival of interest in the political aspects of Nietzsche's thought. Indeed, Keith Ansell-Pearson argues that we cannot begin to understand Nietzsche's thought without considering the role of the political.[127] Over-emphasis on the individual, Ansell-Pearson suggests, has lead to the mistaken impression that Nietzsche's thought is compatible with liberal individualism.[128] On the contrary, says Ansell-Pearson, Nietzsche argues that the point of a political system is to encourage culture and the production of great individuals.[129] This goal requires a form of aristocracy led by philosopher-legislators.[130] On this "great politics" reading of Nietzsche, philosopher-legislators will legislate new values and use their power to further culture and create a race of super-humans.[131]

In further contrast to Kaufmann and Danto, Ansell-Pearson takes the central problem to be the relationship between the individual and society.[132] The opportunity to consider this relationship arises due to the crisis of authority created by nihilism.[133] However, it is this very same crisis of authority that stands in the way of Nietzsche's great politics project. According to Ansell-Pearson, Nietzsche's project requires overcoming the idea that politics serves the ends of morality. He seeks to replace them with the aesthetic project of creating a race of super-humans.[134] Nietzsche attempts this replacement by undermining the metaphysical and supernatural foundations of morality. But, Ansell-Pearson observes, this project involves an appeal to us as beings constituted by the very morality Nietzsche is trying to undermine. Central to Nietzsche's great politics project, then, is the self-overcoming of morality.

[127] Ansell-Pearson (1994), 11, 97.
[128] Ansell-Pearson (1994), 9.
[129] Ansell-Pearson (1994), 120, 129.
[130] Ansell-Pearson (1994), 7, 50-52, 129, 148, 151.
[131] Ansell-Pearson (1994), 120, 147-148.
[132] Ansell-Pearson (1994), 97.
[133] Ansell-Pearson (1994), 8, 102, 147, 204.
[134] Ansell-Pearson (1994), 120.

It's not clear, however, where Nietzsche's deeply immoral philosopher-legislators are meant to get authority for this project.[135] The problem of self-overcoming, then, appears even on this political reading of Nietzsche.

In his *Nietzsche and the Political*, Daniel Conway also explores the political in Nietzsche. Like Ansell-Pearson, Conway sees Nietzsche as arguing that it is the point of politics to cultivate great individuals.[136] Such individuals justify the continued existence of the human race.[137] It is through their experiments in living and heroic exploits that they redeem humanity.[138] However, Nietzsche recognized that modern political institutions were incapable of pursuing such goals. This political incapacity is simply a manifestation of the decline of culture in the modern era.[139] Rather than state legislation, Conway argues, Nietzsche turns to a perfectionist moral self-legislation.[140] Such self-legislation, Nietzsche hopes, will serve as a model and a temptation to others to aspire to human greatness.[141] Nietzsche's political revolution, Conway explains, will take place on a local level, centered around self-legislating individuals.[142] Though Conway's turn to the moral avoids Ansell-Pearson's crisis of authority, his turn to moral perfectionism renders his view, like Kaufmann's, unable to make sense of overcoming.

David Owen puts a twist on the political reading of Nietzsche in his *Nietzsche, Politics & Modernity*. Rather than advocating a particular political system, Owen reads Nietzsche as leveling a critique directed at liberalism.[143] According to this

---

[135]Ansell-Pearson (1994), 102, 132, 154.
[136]Conway (1996), 2-4, 6, 18-26.
[137]Conway (1996), 7.
[138]Conway (1996), 7, 9, 12-13.
[139]Conway (1996), 43-47, 55.
[140]Conway (1996), 55, 61, 63, 68, 74, 80.
[141]Conway (1996), 80-81.
[142]Conway (1996), 85-98.
[143]Owen (1995), 4.

critique, liberalism is an obstacle to the existence of noble individuals in the modern era.[144] Owen provides an interpretation of the *Genealogy of Morals* on which Nietzsche undermines the conception of reason and the abstract individual which are central to liberalism.[145] This genealogical project is meant to display our development into modern individuals such that we can critically reflect on ourselves and, ideally, overcome liberalism.[146]

Key to Nietzsche's project, on Owen's reading, are the characters of the last man and the overman (the Übermensch). Owen claims these are the two human types Nietzsche thinks possible in the modern era.[147] The last man is meant to be the pitiful product of nihilistic liberalism whereas the overman is meant to be the noble individual possible only as the result of the overcoming of liberalism.[148] Elsewhere Owen argues that the persuasive power of the overman is due to our commitment to the Enlightenment ideal of self-government.[149] What makes the overman attractive is precisely his capacity to set his own goals and pursue them whereas the liberal last man lacks goals and integrity.[150] As such, the overman is meant to induce us to overcome liberalism.[151] According to this interpretation, the aim of genealogy is to free us from a particular perspective in order to prepare us for revaluation and overcoming, but again in what self-overcoming consists remains unclear.[152]

Robert Pippin's interpretation of genealogy in his *Nietzsche, Psychology & First Philosophy* parallels Owen's. Genealogy is meant to free us from a particular

---

[144]Owen (1995), 8-9, 133.
[145]Owen (1995), 9, 27-28, 33, 138.
[146]Owen (1995), 39, 54, Cf. Owen (2003).
[147]Owen (1995), 105.
[148]Owen (1995), 105, 111, 122-123, 125.
[149]Owen (1999), esp. 3, 25-27.
[150]Owen (1995), 123, Owen (1999), 25-26.
[151]Owen (1995), 128, Cf. Owen (1999), 25, 27.
[152]Cf. Owen (2002), Owen (2003).

perspective or picture. However, Pippin believes the target is our Christian-moral commitments.[153] Pippin reorients the discussion by taking seriously Nietzsche's insistence that he is engaging in psychology. What this amounts to, Pippin argues, is an interest in the origin and force of our values.[154] Pippin suggests that the problem of nihilism is a lack of desire resulting from a decline in our "erotic attachment" to our values.[155] Nietzsche's project, then, is one of identifying a solution to this "collective failure of desire."[156] The solution lies in achieving freedom via self-overcoming which allows one to identify with one's values and actions.[157] Pippin argues, however, that the project of overcoming requires certain social and historical conditions which are not under the control of the individual.[158] Instead of providing a solution to the problem of nihilism, Pippin claims, Nietzsche offers us methods of enduring its debilitating effects.[159]

## NIETZSCHE AS CULTURE CRITIC

Nietzsche has been interpreted as a moral philosopher, a political philosopher, and as both at the same time. These interpretations, however, often fail to fit the various aspects of Nietzsche's thought together. As we saw in Kaufmann, focusing on the moral led him to awkwardly interpret Nietzsche's political comments as indirectly about the individual. Ansell-Pearson makes no effort to incorporate Nietzsche's comments on philosophy or science. Owen's cast of Nietzsche's work as a critique of liberalism can only awkwardly account for his comments on Christianity, philosophy,

---

[153]Pippin (2010), 29, 45.
[154]Pippin (2010), 20, 26, 29.
[155]Pippin (2010), 29, 39, 53-56.
[156]Pippin (2010), 69.
[157]Pippin (2010), 106-113, 119, Pippin (2009), 79-80, 85.
[158]Pippin (2010), 120, Pippin (2009), 83, 85-86.
[159]Pippin (2010), 116-117.

or science. Further, none of these interpretations is able to give a coherent and non-metaphorical account of overcoming.

Nietzsche is infamous for being the nihilist philosopher who announced the death of God. There is a tendency in Nietzsche interpretation, as we see in Danto, to take Nietzsche's announcement as an urgent insistence that we give up our Christian morality and any other beliefs or judgments that rest on putative metaphysical or supernatural grounds.[160] This is Nietzsche's supposed perspectivism. Though these beliefs give our lives meaning, according to this reading, Nietzsche tells us that these beliefs are groundless and therefore false. Nihilism is the result of realizing the groundlessness of these beliefs. Without these beliefs that give our lives meaning, the best we can hope for is to find some means of enduring our existence.[161]

As we saw above, Danto's reading turns on the falsehood of our beliefs and judgments. However, Nietzsche doesn't take falsehood to be ground for rejecting a belief or judgment. In *Beyond Good & Evil*, for instance, Nietzsche says, "The falseness of a judgment is for us not necessarily an objection to a judgment... The question is to what extent it is life-promoting, life-preserving, species-preserving, perhaps even species-cultivating."[162] Nietzsche may believe that our beliefs and judgments are, strictly speaking, false, but this is irrelevant to the question of whether we should retain them. Indeed, Nietzsche insists that "the falsest judgments... are the most indispensable for us" and if we were to renounce them that "would mean renouncing life and a denial of life."[163] Our lives are such that we need some beliefs and judgments. Nietzsche's critique of Christian morality must rest on something other than the nonexistence of God.

---

[160]Cf. Danto (2005), 12-17, 80.
[161]Cf. Danto (2005), 29, 173-174.
[162]Nietzsche (1992a), 201.
[163]Nietzsche (1992a), 201.

Examination of his criticism of Christian morality reveals that Nietzsche doesn't object to Christianity as a whole, but rather its modern variant. In comparing the Old and New Testaments, he says, "all honor to the Old Testament! I find in it great human beings, a heroic landscape, and something of the very rarest quality in the world, the incomparable naïveté of the *strong heart*..."[164] Such great human beings are absent from the New Testament. Nietzsche notes a parallel development in our conception of God. "Formerly," he says, "he [God] represented a people, the strength of a people, everything aggressive and thirsting for power in the soul of a people: now he is merely a good God..."[165] What is objectionable about Christianity, then, is not its falsehood or its supernatural foundations, but something about its modern variant.

Nietzsche objects to the modern variant of Christianity because it is characterized by a morality of pity. Such pity, he claims, is hostile to life.[166] "God," he says, has "degenerated to the *contradiction of life*...a declaration of hostility towards life..."[167] But Christianity is not the only place in which Nietzsche sees this modern penchant for pity. He insists it permeates all aspects of modern life.[168] He sees it in the social and political institutions of the modern era, in the rise of democracy and equality.[169] Speaking in *Beyond Good & Evil* of the democratic movement in Europe, Nietzsche says, "behind all the moral and political foregrounds...a tremendous *physiological* process is taking place and gaining momentum."[170] He sees it reflected in the philosophy of his day, which he insists is primarily directed at providing ad

---

[164]Nietzsche (1992b), 580.
[165]Nietzsche (1968a), 126, Cf. Nietzsche (1992b), 526.
[166]Nietzsche (1968a), 118-119.
[167]Nietzsche (1968a), 128, Cf. Nietzsche (1969), 73.
[168]Nietzsche (1968a), 117, 120.
[169]Nietzsche (1992a), 306, Nietzsche (1968b), 91, Nietzsche (1968a), 156.
[170]Nietzsche (1992a), 366.

hoc justifications for the judgments we accept uncritically.[171] Nietzsche also sees this pity on display in Darwin's theory of evolution, which holds up the mediocre mass as the acme of human development.[172] These values, he claims, are the values of declining life—of decadence.[173]

The whole of modernity is characterized by pity and the values of decadence. But this is not Nietzsche's central claim. Rather, he says, "Our softening of customs—this is my thesis, my *innovation* if you like—is a consequence of decline; stern and frightful customs can, conversely, be a consequence of a superabundance of life."[174] Nietzsche's central insight, then, is that the cultural decline of modernity signals a general decline of life, vitality, or health.[175] Modern man is sick.[176]

If this is right then understanding Nietzsche requires that we make sense of his claim that modern man is sick. Danto insists that it is unclear what he means by this.[177] Contra Danto, I suggest we take seriously Nietzsche's claim that he is engaged in a physio-psychological investigation.[178] This approach is similar in spirit to Pippin's suggestion that we consider Nietzsche's thought as a psychological investigation. The difference lies in giving equal emphasis to the role the body plays. The very idea of sickness suggests the body plays an important role in Nietzsche's thought.

There is significant textual evidence to support this physio-psychological reading. In *The Anti-Christ* Nietzsche insists that Christianity requires individuals who

---

[171]Nietzsche (1992a), 200, 202-204, 287, Nietzsche (1968b), 35-39.
[172]Nietzsche (1968b), 75-76, Nietzsche (1968a), 124, Nietzsche (1992b), 478-480, Nietzsche (1969), 138.
[173]Nietzsche (1968a), 117.
[174]Nietzsche (1968b), 90.
[175]Cf. Conway (1996), 45.
[176]Nietzsche (1968b), 115.
[177]Danto (2005), 170-171.
[178]Nietzsche (1992a), 221.

are both physically and intellectually sick or weak.[179] In *Twilight of the Idols* Nietzsche suggests that the idea of sin or guilt is simply an interpretation "foisted upon a physiological discomfort."[180] In *Beyond Good & Evil* he describes pleasure and pain as "mere epiphenomena" of having or lacking power.[181] In *Genealogy of Morals* power is described in physio-psychological terms as the feeling accompanying an expenditure of strength.[182] Indeed, physicality, life, strength and weakness, health and illness are motifs present throughout Nietzsche's analysis of values and culture.

This physio-psychological analysis reveals a dynamic relationship between culture and the individual. A culture preserves and promotes certain kinds of individuals by means of its particular moral valuations.[183] These moral valuations are interpretations of our physio-psychological experiences or characteristics.[184] Nietzsche tells us that there are two kinds of morality: noble and slave morality.[185] The difference between these two moralities is their respective valuation of power and strength.[186] Central to noble morality is a positive valuation of power and strength.[187] Slave morality, on the other hand, gives a negative valuation of these characteristics. Nietzsche argues that slave morality, which makes power and strength into an evil, developed out of hatred and resentment of the nobles.[188] By making power and strength a moral fault the weaker class are able to exert power over the stronger class.

The particular moral valuations of a culture have long-term consequences

---

[179]Nietzsche (1968a), 167, 169.
[180]Nietzsche (1968b), 52, Cf. Nietzsche (1992b), 565.
[181]Nietzsche (1992a), 343.
[182]Nietzsche (1992b), 543.
[183]Nietzsche (1969), 84, Nietzsche (1992a), 287-290.
[184]Nietzsche (1992a), 201, Nietzsche (1992b), 565.
[185]Nietzsche (1992a), 394-398.
[186]Nietzsche (1992b), 476.
[187]Nietzsche (1992b), 462.
[188]Nietzsche (1992b), 472-475.

on the physio-psychological constitution of the individuals of that culture. These valuations preserve and promote certain physio-psychological kinds of individuals. Modern culture is characterized by a Christian morality of pity, which is a type of slave morality. Modern culture has, thereby, encouraged a weak kind of individual to prosper. The predominance of Christian morality, Nietzsche insists, has created "a smaller, almost ridiculous type, a herd animal, something eager to please, sickly, and mediocre has been bred, the European of today."[189] The weak and sick men of modernity, then, are the result of a culture characterized by a slave morality.[190]

Nietzsche tells us that the truth or falsity of a judgment is not a basis for rejecting that judgment. Rather, the "question is to what extent it is life-promoting, life-preserving, species-preserving, perhaps even species-cultivating."[191] While we cannot judge a culture on the truth or falsity of its judgments, we can ask whether it promotes life. "Life" in the sense in which Nietzsche uses it refers to a physio-psychological process characterized by suffering. Healthy and happy individuals are those with the strength to endure and embrace the suffering which accompanies living. Nietzsche identifies the Dionysian Hellenes as one such people. The Hellenes, according to Nietzsche, were able *"realize in onself* the eternal joy of becoming—that joy which also encompasses *joy in destruction. . ."*[192] He isn't interested in the survival of large numbers of individuals, but in the quality of the individual's life.[193] An abundance of strong, healthy, and happy individuals signals a good, ascending culture.

A culture in decline, on the other hand, is indicated by an abundance of weak,

---

[189]Nietzsche (1992a), 266.

[190]Cf. Nietzsche (1968a), 127, Nietzsche (1992a), 366.

[191]Nietzsche (1992a), 201.

[192]Nietzsche (1968b), 110, Cf. Nietzsche (1992a), 254.

[193]Nietzsche (1968b), 98, Nietzsche (1992a), 211. It is unclear whether Danto understands that Nietzsche is not using the term "life" in this way. Cf. Danto (2005), 126-127.

sick, and unhappy individuals. Sick and unhappy individuals are those without the strength to endure and embrace suffering. Weak individuals, Nietzsche claims, look for ways of living which promise to eradicate suffering.[194] The Christian morality of pity has provided such a way of living.[195] Christianity teaches one to deny the body, instincts, and passions.[196] In effect, Nietzsche argues, modern Christian life is like unto a kind of living death.[197] It solves the problem of life—suffering—by teaching us to live in a way that denies that life is a bodied experience characterized by suffering. The life of modern man, Nietzsche says, is a "physiological self-contradiction."[198]

Though we cannot judge a culture on its claim to truth, we can judge it according to the kind of individuals it produces. Modernity, Nietzsche observes, is characterized by an abundance of weak and sick individuals and a dearth of strong characters.[199] "Great men," he says "are explosive material... there has been no explosion for a long time."[200] Modern culture is in decline. The valuations of modernity fail to give meaning to our suffering. Instead, modernity is characterized by a way of life that denies life. The valuations of modernity must be rejected because they fail to help us endure and embrace life. Moreover, these moral valuations contribute to the problem because they preserve and promote weak kinds of individuals.

Nietzsche's announcement that God has died, then, is the announcement that the way of life centered around the ideal of God no longer serves its function. Modern culture fails to help the modern man make sense of his life and its characteristic suffering. While God used to inspire stories of strong individuals, in the modern

---

[194]Nietzsche (1968b), 30, 45, Nietzsche (1992b), 503, Nietzsche (1969), 59-61.
[195]Nietzsche (1968a), 151.
[196]Nietzsche (1968a), 125, 155-156, 162-163, Cf. Nietzsche (1968b), 34, 42, Nietzsche (1992a), 251, 343.
[197]Cf. Nietzsche (1992b), 503, Nietzsche (1968b), 42, Nietzsche (1969), 73.
[198]Nietzsche (1968b), 95, Cf. Nietzsche (1992b), 553, 556.
[199]Nietzsche (1969), 300.
[200]Nietzsche (1968b), 97.

era he has become the idol of the weak.[201] The values of pity in evidence in the politics, philosophy, and science of late nineteenth century Europe signal a physio-psychological decline. What we need in order to reverse the trend of decline is a new ideal and a fundamental shift of our valuations toward a noble morality.[202] Nietzsche prescribes the Übermensch and a new noble moral valuation.[203]

## THE NIETZSCHEAN INDIVIDUAL

It was stated above that Nietzsche sees a dynamic relationship between culture and the individual. So far, only the effect of culture on the individual has been explored. The problem of nihilism in the modern era, however, requires that individuals affect—indeed, affect a revolution in—culture. Nietzsche insists the culture of the modern era needs to be replaced. We need to change the valuations of our culture. The question, as several commentators point out, is whether the individual can do this.

Nietzsche recognizes the difficulty of this problem. In *Thus Spoke Zarathustra*, Zarathustra asks his fellow higher men, "Who could overturn with reasons what the mob has once learned to believe without reasons?"[204] Speaking to the Stoics in *Beyond Good & Evil*, Nietzsche says, "For all your love of truth, you have forced yourselves so long, so persistently, so rigidly-hypnotically to see nature the wrong way, namely Stoically, that you are no longer able to see her differently..."[205] This is especially the case with Christian morality. Modern man, Nietzsche notes, increasingly rejects God and the tenets of Christianity and yet continues to live in

---

[201]Cf. Nietzsche (1969), 272-273, Nietzsche (1968a), 162-163.
[202]Nietzsche (1992a), 234-235.
[203]Nietzsche (1969), 297, Nietzsche (1992a), 258.
[204]Nietzsche (1969), 300.
[205]Nietzsche (1992a), 206.

accordance with Christian moral values.[206] The decadent values of modernity are so persistent because modern man is a product of the culture of modernity.

The key is that Nietzsche doesn't look to the modern man to carry out this cultural revival. Instead, he looks to the new philosopher. The new philosopher is the diasporic class of individuals with the strength and ability to carry out a cultural revival. But Nietzsche is at turns hesitant and insistent about their appearance. In *Thus Spoke Zarathustra*, Zarathustra looks to the higher men to "write upon new law-tables the word: 'Noble'."[207] At the end of the story, the higher men accept a donkey as their God and Zarathustra wonders "Who shall be master of the world?"[208] At one point in *Beyond Good & Evil*, Nietzsche is adamant, "Toward *new philosophers*; there is no choice...," but later he reprises his hesitancy, "And to ask it one more: today—is greatness *possible?*"[209] He is again insistent in the *Genealogy of Morals* saying, "—*he must come one day*—."[210] This waffling reflects Nietzsche's desperation for a cultural revival as well as his pessimism that it will occur. He thinks that if a reversal of our valuations is to occur it will only be as a result of the efforts of the new philosophers—our Nietzschean individual.[211]

Though his hesitance and pessimism is evident, Nietzsche is hopeful. His hope lies in his belief that the conditions of the modern era are perfect for the appearance of the Nietzschean individual. He believes that precisely the social conditions which serve to exacerbate the decline in modern culture provide the opportunity for its reversal. The higher and weaker types of men, he says, "belong together and owe

---

[206]Nietzsche (1968a), 149-150, Nietzsche (1968b), 527, Nietzsche (1992a), 259-261.
[207]Nietzsche (1969), 220.
[208]Nietzsche (1969), 329.
[209]Nietzsche (1992a), 307, 329.
[210]Nietzsche (1992b), 532.
[211]Cf. Nietzsche (1992b), 561.

their origins to the same causes."[212] The modern era has seen an increase in cross-cultural reproduction. Such "inter-breeding" of the peoples of Europe, Nietzsche thinks, has created individuals in which various and conflicting cultural valuations compete. The resulting internal conflict unsettles the influence of culture:

> The past of every form and way of life, or cultures that formerly lay right next to each other or one on top of the other, now flows into us 'modern souls,' thanks to this mixture; our instincts now run back everywhere; we ourselves are a kind of chaos.[213]

This cultural confusion, then, creates individuals who experience internal confusion. Their instincts, their bodies, and sensibilities have not been irreversibly shaped by any one culture.[214]

Without a coherent culture to shape them these individuals are in a unique position. The majority of these individuals will succumb to the confusion and join the weak mass. But Nietzsche thinks a few individuals will have the strength to impose their own order and valuations on the chaos of their instincts.[215] Such individuals, Nietzsche believes, will take advantage of the tension of their souls created by these competing valuations.[216] They will overcome themselves by imposing order on the chaos of their instincts and, thereby, create new valuations.

Overcoming, then, consists in providing an alternate interpretation, a new moral valuation, an order to the chaos of one's own physio-psychological experience and characteristics. But not any new interpretation will do. Nietzsche offers the Übermensch as an ideal to center the valuations of the Nietzschean individuals. This ideal embodies the characteristics of the noble individual. The Übermensch is the

[212]Nietzsche (1992a), 302.
[213]Nietzsche (1992a), 341.
[214]Nietzsche (1992a), 301-302.
[215]Cf. Nietzsche (1992b), 488.
[216]Nietzsche (1992b), 521, Nietzsche (1992a), 193.

strong human animal who creates values.[217] A culture centered on such an ideal should preserve and promote strong and noble individuals.

What Nietzsche envisioned as the relationship between the Nietzschean individuals and the rest of society is not obvious. It is clear that Nietzsche does not think everyone can be a noble individual. The class of noble individuals require "a broad base... a strongly and soundly consolidated mediocrity."[218] The weak mass cannot be eradicated because the noble class needs them.[219] Some commentators read this as evidence advocating an aristocracy centered around noble individuals. Indeed, the Nietzchean individual is particularly politicized in *Beyond Good & Evil*. "*Genuine philosophers*," Nietzsche says, "*are commanders and legislators*: they say, '*thus* it *shall* be!' "[220]

This politicized rendering of the philosopher-legislator, however, is out of place in the rest of Nietzsche's works. He frequently encourages the higher types to seek solitude. For instance, in expounding on the concept of the noble, Nietzsche says, "solitude is a virtue for us... All community makes men—somehow, somewhere, sometime 'common.' "[221] The process of overcoming, then, is a process of self-legislating, a process of imposing form and creating valuations on one's own physio-psychological experience and characteristics. In describing the Nietzschean individual, Nietzsche seems to have in mind a philosopher-hermit, like Zarathustra. Indeed, the one manifestation of the ascetic ideal of which Nietzsche approves occurs in philosophers. In the solitude and self-discipline encouraged by the ascetic ideal, the philosopher finds the "optimum of favorable conditions under which it can expend

---

[217]Nietzsche (1992a), 258.
[218]Nietzsche (1968a), 179.
[219]Cf. Nietzsche (1969), 215.
[220]Nietzsche (1992a), 326.
[221]Nietzsche (1992a), 416, Cf. Nietzsche (1969), 77, Nietzsche (1992a), 275, 412, Nietzsche (1992b), 545, 561, 572.

its strength and achieve its maximal feeling of power..."[222] Though Nietzsche was likely attracted to the idea of philosopher-legislators, the bulk of his discussion on this topic indicates an individual self-legislating and creating new values for herself.

This is not to say that the upshot of Nietzsche's work is to encourage individuals to go live in caves and keep their new values only for themselves. He clearly envisions the activities of the Nietzschean individual as having far-reaching cultural implications. In *Thus Spoke Zarathustra* he has Zarathustra say, "The world revolves about the inventor of new values: imperceptibly it revolves."[223] By creating new values and a new culture around the ideal of the Übermensch, Nietzschean individuals will also recreate humankind. But the task of creating a new culture and, thereby, recreating humankind will require generations of effort.[224] In the meantime, Nietzsche is fervently calling on these individuals, desperately encouraging them to continue being great in an era dominated by the weak.[225] The fate of humankind, he warns, depends on it.

Central to Nietzsche's appeal to the Nietzschean individual is the idea that human beings are creative animals. We are animals in the sense that we are physio-psychological beings. We are bodied. We have instincts and passions. But we are also creative in that we interpret our physio-psychological experiences and characteristics. We provide a moral valuation of the physio-psychological which permeates our culture. Through this valuation we preserve and promote a particular kind of life and particular kinds of individuals. Individuals are products of their culture, but culture is, ultimately, a human creation. Thus, in order to overcome and, thereby,

---

[222]Nietzsche (1992b), 543-544, Cf. Nietzsche (1992b), 548-550.
[223]Nietzsche (1969), 78, Cf. 153-154.
[224]Nietzsche (1968b), 100-101.
[225]It is interesting to compare John Stuart Mill's project in *On Liberty* with Nietzsche's. While Mill appeals to the mass to allow the exemplary the freedom to be exemplary, Nietzsche, perhaps more realistically, appeals to the exemplary to have the courage to continue to be exemplary.

carry out a cultural revival, the Nietzschean individuals have to recognize that we are creative animals.[226] They have to become what they are.[227]

This is where Nietzsche's insistence that there is no supernatural or metaphysical truth becomes important. As he notes, the grip of Christian morality is difficult to escape because it denies the possibility of other interpretations.[228] Its putative supernatural foundations rule out competing claims to truth and its rejection of the body, the senses, and the empirical rule out potential contrary evidence.[229] His persistent reminders that all interpretations are false, then, are meant to free us from the grip of Christian morality.[230] Nietzsche's point is that the valuations of this morality are damaging, but there is nothing necessary about them. They are only one of many interpretations that we can construct.[231] In denying supernatural and metaphysical truth, Nietzsche means to bring to our attention our nature as creators. "In man," he says, "*creature* and *creator* are united..."[232] Rather than committing us to the fate of nihilism, as Danto suggests, Nietzsche's rejection of objective truth frees us to create new valuations and give meaning to our lives for ourselves.

On Nietzsche's physio-psychological analysis of culture, modern man is in a state of decline. Broadly, the problem Nietzsche sees is that the culture of late nineteenth century Europe does not help individuals make sense of their lives. This is the same kind of problem as that facing our individual caught in a moment of culture crisis. Nietzsche looks to the new philosopher—our Nietzschean individual—to resolve this problem. He hopes the Nietzschean individual will carry out a cultural

---

[226]Nietzsche (1992b), 506.
[227]Nietzsche (1969), 252.
[228]Nietzsche1968a, 120.
[229]Nietzsche (1968a), 164-165.
[230]Cf. Nietzsche (1992a), 201, 212, 219, 235-236, Nietzsche (1968b), 36.
[231]Nietzsche (1992a), 249, 287-288, Nietzsche (1992b), 515.
[232]Nietzsche (1992a), 344.

revival through the process of overcoming. In order to resolve the problem of culture crisis in her own case, then, our individual must be a Nietzschean individual. She must overcome and provide herself with new interpretation and moral valuation.

This chapter opened with a survey of interpretation of Nietzsche's thought. It was argued that these different interpretations suffered from common difficulties and failed to give a coherent account of overcoming. In order to address these common interpretive problems, I offered an alternate physio-psychological reading. This physio-psychological interpretation took seriously Nietzsche's talk about health, strength, and power and focused on the dynamic relationship between human beings and culture.

According to this physio-psychological interpretation, Nietzsche literally means that modern man is sick. Modern culture fails to give man the means to endure and embrace the suffering characteristic of life. It fails to help modern man make sense of his life. To resolve this problem Nietzsche looks to the Nietzschean individual to engage in overcoming and, thereby, to carry out a cultural revival. Overcoming involves giving form and order to the chaos of one's instincts by providing a new interpretation of physio-psychological experiences and characteristics. This account of overcoming remains highly metaphorical. The next chapter will develop a non-metaphorical account of overcoming by looking to Nietzsche's view of the nature of language.

# MAKING SENSE OF NIETZSCHE

Though there is wide variety in Nietzsche interpretation, few commentators have concentrated on his philosophy of language. An implication of the physio-psychological analysis of Nietzsche's thought presented in the previous chapter is that the notion of overcoming is central to his thought. As the Nietzschean individual is supposed to carry out Nietzsche's hoped-for cultural revival by engaging in overcoming, Nietzsche's project rests on the coherence of this idea. More importantly for our purposes, the fate of our individual caught in a moment of culture crisis relies on overcoming. We must, then, find a non-metaphorical account of this notion.

This chapter will suggest that Nietzsche's philosophy of language is essential to this task. However, Nietzsche's lack of prowess in the philosophy of language has left his thought open to allegedly debilitating criticism such as Danto's. In contrast, Maudemarie Clark gives an extensive defense of the development of Nietzsche's thought on language and truth. Unfortunately, this defense gets the character of Nietzsche's view wrong and ends up deflating Nietzsche just as Danto set out to do. After examining Clark's defense, this chapter will argue that we need something like a Wittgensteinian view of language in order to make sense of Nietzsche's idea of overcoming.

## NIETZSCHE AS A NEO-KANTIAN

As was seen in the previous chapter, Athur Danto attempts to deflate and demythologize Nietzsche by showing that his view involves an internal contradiction. According to Danto's interpretation of Nietzsche's perspectivist theory of truth, all our beliefs and judgments are, strictly speaking, false. There are no metaphysical or supernatural grounds that privilege any system of beliefs or judgments over another. As these beliefs and judgments are false we have no right to them. Danto's Nietzsche encourages the individual to free herself from these beliefs and judgments and, thereby, unleash her antisocial passions. The problem, says Danto, is that Nietzsche's perspectivism renders this move impossible. There is no perspective from which the individual can criticize the collective perspective.[233]

This perspectivist theory of truth poses an additional problem for Nietzsche as it renders the status of his claims unclear. It seems as though his perspectivism amounts to the claim that there is no truth and that is the truth. This is a plain contradiction. Nietzsche can attempt to avoid this contradiction by forwarding a weaker perspectivist claim. On this weaker version, the claim is just an articulation of Nietzsche's own perspective. However, this weaker version makes it unclear why we should find his claims compelling. Consider his critique of Christianity. Nietzsche says we should abandon modern Christian moral values because they are not life-affirming. However, according to the weaker version of his perspectivism, this is just Nietzsche's perspective. That Nietzsche has these opinions about Christianity has no necessary implications for us.[234] Nietzsche's perspectivism, then, seems to pose two serious problems for his thought.

---

[233]Danto (2005), 119-127, Clark (1990), 1-3.
[234]Cf. Clark (1990), 3-4. Clark (1990), 151.

I suggested in the previous chapter that this reading of perspectivism is a mis-interpretation of Nietzsche. This chapter will present a more sustained argument. This argument will focus on the work of Maudemarie Clark, a student of Danto's, who presents a more developed version of his reading in her 1990 *Nietzsche on Truth and Philosophy*. Though Clark defends Nietzsche, her argument depends on Danto's interpretation. She agrees with Danto that Nietzsche's early perspectivism undermines his project. However, she argues that Nietzsche's view on truth only takes final form after *Beyond Good & Evil*. She characterizes his mature perspectivism as a kind of neo-Kantian view of truth, which, she argues, allows him to avoid the problems that plague his early views.

*On Truth and Lies in a Nonmoral Sense* is a 1873 essay by Nietzsche. It is one of his most extensive treatments of the topic of truth and the nature of language. In this essay Nietzsche likens truths to illusions. Clark argues that this assertion commits him to the claim that all beliefs that we call "true" are actually false. "He must mean," says Clark, "that we are mistaken concerning the beliefs we call 'true,' that these beliefs are false rather than true... To deny this is to reject logic."[235] The difference between truth and lies, Nietzsche explains, is not a matter of truth or falsehood, but rather of social convention. If a statement conforms to conventions, it is true. If not, it is false.[236] According to this view, there are no truths, but only socially accepted and sanctioned conventions. This is Danto's perspectivism.

Nietzsche's rejection of truth rests upon a view of language as metaphor. Regarding this view of language, Nietzsche says:

> ... we believe that we know something about the things themselves when
> we speak of trees, colors, snow, and flowers; and yet we possess nothing

---

[235]Clark (1990), 66.
[236]Clark (1990), 67.

but metaphors for things—metaphors which correspond in no way to the original entities.[237]

Though we think we are speaking about the constituents of the world, our concepts are only metaphors for things in the world. Our beliefs are not and cannot be true because our language does not correspond directly with the things in the world.

Clark argues, however, that this view of language is not sufficient for Nietzsche's rejection of truth. This rejection requires two further premises. The first is a representational theory of perception according to which we do not perceive the world in a direct and unmediated fashion.[238] The second premise is a metaphysical correspondence theory of truth according to which a proposition is true if and only if it corresponds to things-in-themselves.[239]

Taken together, Clark argues, these three premises lead Nietzsche to what Clark refers to as the "falsification thesis." According to the falsification thesis our beliefs falsify reality. It amounts, Clark says, "to calling the empirical world, the world accessible through common sense and science, illusory or fictitious."[240] Our beliefs are not true because our concepts do not correspond to things-in-themselves. Further, our beliefs cannot be true because all our evidence about things-in-themselves is distorted.[241]

---

[237]Nietzsche (1979), 82-83.

[238]Cf. Danto (2005), 27-35. It is actually unclear if Nietzsche is committed to this. Nietzsche comments about perception, "What is a word? It is the copy in sound of a nerve stimulus. But the further inference from the nerve stimulus to a cause outside of us is already the result of a false and unjustifiable application of the principle of sufficient reason." Nietzsche (1979), 81. Nietzsche seems to be suggesting that we do not have grounds to decide about the relationship between our sense evidence and the external world. Clark's gloss takes Nietzsche to assume that our sense evidence distorts reality. This gloss, however, is clearly in tension with Nietzsche's advocacy of epistemological agnosticism. In addition, it is interesting to compare Nietzsche with Russell on this topic. If Nietzsche is an agnostic, Russell seems to be an evangelic.

[239]Clark (1990), 77-85.

[240]Clark (1990), 114.

[241]It is not obvious that this is what Nietzsche means by his comments on our senses. More on this later.

Clark claims that Nietzsche's rejection of truth is a result of his failure to suppose there might be a non-metaphysical account of truth.[242] Clark argues that Nietzsche ultimately rejects the metaphysical correspondence theory of truth because it relies on the concept of the thing-in-itself.[243] If truth were independent of our cognitive interests, then it would depend upon the structure of reality—the thing-in-itself—independently of our interests and concepts. On such a view, truth might be completely inaccessible to us. In that case we would be unable to conceive of the thing-in-itself. But a concept that cannot be conceived is a contradiction. This rejection of the thing-in-itself lays the foundation for his mature perspectivism, which, Clark argues, amounts to a denial that truth is independent of our interests and concepts.[244]

Clark argues that the later Nietzsche realized—or should have realized—that his objection to a metaphysical conception of truth does not commit him to rejecting truth all together. She notes that it is unclear whether the later Nietzsche realized this, but nonetheless argues that if there is no thing-in-itself there is nothing for our beliefs to falsify. Further, she claims, there is no evidence of the falsification thesis in his works after *Beyond Good & Evil*. We see "no claim that the human world is a falsification, no claim that science, logic, or mathematics falsify reality."[245] Indeed, she says, the later Nietzsche is a friend of common sense and science. If there

---

[242]Clark (1990), 83.

[243]Clark argues that, at bottom, Nietzsche rejects the metaphysical because it "expresses the nihilistic ascetic ideal." Clark (1990), 23. According to Clark's Nietzsche the metaphysically-centered perspective of the ascetic ideal should be rejected because it "no longer encourages widespread self-discipline or restraint" and has "stripped life of any intrinsic value." Clark (1990), 166. This reading of the terms "life-affirming" or "life-promoting" as benefitting "human life in general" by promoting peace, undermining aggression, promoting survival of the greatest number, and avoiding mass depression understandably parallel's Danto's reading, but as was suggested in the previous chapter this reading is not true to Nietzsche's meaning. Cf. Clark (1990), 163-165.

[244]Clark (1990), 50-61.

[245]Clark (1990), 103, Cf. 105.

is no independent metaphysical reality, she observes, the absence of metaphysical truth implies nothing for science or our common sense beliefs. A common sense or "minimal correspondence conception" of truth is consistent with his objections to metaphysics.[246] It is the presence of these two conceptions of truth—common sense and metaphysical—that leads Clark to characterize Nietzsche as a neo-Kantian.[247]

Clark attributes to Nietzsche a neo-Kantian view of truth in order to save his view from the serious problems of the perspectivism attributed to him by Danto. However, though she sets out to argue that Nietzsche *is* a neo-Kantian and *did* maintain a neo-Kantian view of truth in his later works, her argument is largely provisional and speculative. Her argument rests on a lack of contrary evidence and her insistence that her neo-Kantian interpretation is "more plausible" or "obvious" despite noting comments of Nietzsche's that suggest against her reading.[248] She maintains her characterization of Nietzsche as a neo-Kantian despite his persistent criticism of Kant and her own admission that Kant maintained that reality has an independent structure whereas Nietzsche denies this.[249]

Additionally, Clark's interpretation of Nietzsche and his views of language and truth are unable to give us a robust understanding of nihilism and overcoming. As she glosses it, nihilism is a morale problem arising out of the realization that our beliefs and judgments have no metaphysical or supernatural foundation. Without this source of meaning, she says, "it will be difficult to work up a great deal of enthusiasm for living and doing."[250] Overcoming, on her reading, is a process of internalizing the will to power, which she takes to be a desire for power necessary for

---

[246]Clark (1990), 31, 135.

[247]Clark (1990), 22, 31, 103-115, 133-135. The common sense and metaphysical conceptions of truth are meant to roughly map onto Kant's phenomenal and noumenal truth.

[248]Clark (1990), 103, 106, 117-118, 127.

[249]Clark (1990), 61.

[250]Clark (1990), 232.

the affirmation of life.[251] This overcoming will result in our "imagining differences we can make, setting goals, and working towards them..."[252] However, this gloss on nihilism gives no sense of the depth or difficulty of the problem. Its accompanying reading of overcoming gives no hint as to the role of valuation or interpretation. Moreover, her characterization of the later Nietzsche as an advocate of common sense and science robs his thought of the revolutionary and creative character necessary for his hoped-for cultural revival.

Clark's attempt to defend Nietzsche against the problems associated with Danto's reading of his perspectivism is admirable. It is, however, plagued with problems. Moreover, she often seems more interested in saving science and common sense from Nietzsche than saving Nietzsche from Danto's criticisms. The next section will present a defense of Nietzsche of a different nature. Rather than theories of truth and perception, this defense will focus on Nietzsche's comments regarding the nature of language.

## NIETZSCHE ON LANGUAGE

Clark's neo-Kantian defense of Nietzsche depended on a particular reading of his *On Truth and Lies in a Nonmoral Sense*. According to this reading, he rejects truth because he maintains a metaphysical correspondence theory of truth. Against this reading, I will argue that in this essay Nietzsche rejects a particular view of language. The alternate view of language he develops there remains more or less intact throughout the rest of his works. Further, this alternate view of language provides a basis for a coherent account of overcoming as a process which results in

---

[251]Clark (1990), 232, 283.
[252]Clark (1990), 258.

conceptual creation or revision.

Clark takes Nietzsche's claim in *On Truth and Lies in a Nonmoral Sense* that truths are illusions to commit him to the claim that the beliefs and judgments we take to be true are false. Against this reading, I suggest that in likening truths to illusions Nietzsche means that language is not an instrument of science. When we are engaged in scientific investigation, we think we are speaking about the constituents of the world. In our everyday lives, we tend to think that when we utter true sentences we are describing how things stand in the world. This is a highly intuitive view. In likening truths to illusions, however, Nietzsche is asserting that this is not the case.[253] Our language, he says, "if not derived from never-never land, is at least not derived from the essence of things."[254] We tend to think our judgments and beliefs concern the nature of reality, but this gets the nature of language wrong.

Rather than an instrument of science, Nietzsche suggests that language is an instrument of power. Prior to the formation of society, in the war of all against all, Nietzsche claims, individuals used language as a means for self-preservation. It is by means of the "powers of dissimulation" manifested in language use that weaker individuals can preserve themselves against physically stronger individuals.[255] Within society, however, language becomes a means for the smooth operation and continued existence of the collective. With the inception of society, he says, a system of reference and a set of truths is established.[256] Being a member of the society requires using the same system of reference as everyone else. Use of the common language becomes a duty and is enforced with moral sanction.[257]

---

[253]Nietzsche (1979), 82-83.
[254]Nietzsche (1979), 83.
[255]Nietzsche (1979), 80-81.
[256]Nietzsche (1979), 81.
[257]Nietzsche (1979), 84.

We forget that language is an instrument of power rather than an instrument of science. However, we can remind ourselves of the nature of language by looking at a variety of languages. He says:

> The various languages placed side by side show that with words it is never a question of truth, never a question of adequate expression; otherwise, there would not be so many languages.[258]

Looking at many different languages and the different structures of their concepts, we can see that language is not a means of describing the world. Language is not a means of describing the relationships that obtain between things. Nietzsche insists, rather, that language is a means of describing the "relations of things to men" and "a sum of human relations."[259]

The view of language as an instrument of science assumes that our concepts reflect the the structure of the world. It assumes that our concepts correspond to the constituents of reality and that the relationships that obtain between our concepts reflect the relationships between the constituents of reality. But this, says Nietzsche, mistakes the origin and nature of our concepts. He says:

> We obtain the concept, as we do the form, by overlooking what is individual and actual; whereas nature is acquainted with no forms and no concepts, and likewise with no species, but only with an X which remains inaccessible and indefinable for us. For even our contrast between individual and species is something anthropomorphic and does not originate in the essence of things.[260]

Our language is a body of concepts, but these concepts do not reflect the structure of reality, assuming it has one. Rather, Nietzsche explains, our concepts are the result

---

[258]Nietzsche (1979), 82.
[259]Clark (1990), 82, 84.
[260]Nietzsche (1979), 83.

of a multiplicity of metaphors. By "metaphor" he means "the equation of unequal things." In creating and employing concepts, he thinks, we equate or assimilate things that are dissimilar and are even completely different kinds of things such as nerve stimuli and images, images and sounds or words, and different cases of each of these.[261]

Our mistake about the nature of language is a result, Nietzsche argues, of forgetting something about our own nature. It is, Nietzsche says:

> ... only by means of the petrification and coagulation of a mass of images which originally streamed from the primal faculty of human imagination like a fiery liquid, only in the invincible faith that *this* sun, *this* window, *this* table is a truth in itself, in short, only by forgetting that he himself is an *artistically creating* subject, does man live with any repose and consistency.[262]

The appearance that the world has a stable and persisting structure is the result of the concepts that we have created, rather than of the nature of the world itself.

In forwarding this view of language, Nietzsche ultimately is seeking to remind us of our nature as artistically creating subjects. In arguing against the view that language is an instrument of science, Nietzsche is reminding us of our role in the creation and application of concepts. "The drive," he says, "toward the formation of metaphors [concepts] is the fundamental human drive, which one cannot for a single instant dispense with in thought, for one would thereby dispense with man himself."[263] This reminder is meant to free us from our conceptual prison. Speaking of our concepts, he says:

> That immense framework and planking of concepts to which the needy man clings his whole life long in order to preserve himself is nothing

---

[261]Nietzsche (1979), 82-83.
[262]Nietzsche (1979), 86, Cf. 84.
[263]Nietzsche (1979), 88-89.

but a scaffolding and toy for the most audacious feats of the liberated intellect. And when it [the liberated intellect] smashes this framework to pieces, throws it into confusion, and puts it back together in an ironic fashion, pairing the most alien things and separating the closest, it is demonstrating that it has no need of these makeshifts...[264]

The liberated intellect realizes the contingency of concepts and rather than being imprisoned by them, plays with them and creates new ones.[265] Concepts are our own creation, but they imprison us when we forget this fact.[266]

The end of the essay suggests that Nietzsche's aim in reminding us of our nature as artistically creating subjects is to instigate a cultural revival. Nietzsche introduces the intuitive man and the rational man.[267] The rational man is the scientific man, who attains the practical necessities of living through the guidance of our concepts. The intuitive man, on the other hand, realizes the contingency of our concepts and is guided instead by intuition. The life of the intuitive man destroys the conceptual prison and renews the process of concept formation. Different ages, according to Nietzsche, are characterized by the dominance of either the rational man or the intuitive man. Ages dominated by the intuitive man are cultural ages characterized by art, beauty, and happiness.[268]

This reading of Nietzsche's *On Truth and Lies in a Nonmoral Sense* gives a very different impression than Clark's reading. Instead of the topic of truth, this reading takes Nietzsche to be primarily concerned with the nature of language. A consequence of this view of language is that the metaphysical correspondence theory of truth is incorrect. And Nietzsche is aware of this consequence. Part of arguing

---

[264]Nietzsche (1979), 90.
[265]Nietzsche (1979), 89-90.
[266]The reader should compare this with Wittgenstein's idea of entanglement.
[267]Nietzsche (1979), 90.
[268]Nietzsche (1979), 90-91.

against the view of language as an instrument of science requires unsettling this highly intuitive view of truth. Contra Clark, however, Nietzsche's primary aim in this essay is to forward a view of language and reorient our understanding of the relationship between ourselves, language, and the world and thereby instigate a cultural revival.

In fairness to Clark, Nietzsche's comments are at times incautious and he does appear to take a metaphysical correspondence theory of truth as the standard. Our beliefs, he says, are not about "the things themselves" and our language is "not derived from the essence of things."[269] Regarding our ability to point out objects corresponding to our concepts, Nietzsche says, "it is a truth of limited value... a thoroughly anthropomorphic truth which contains not a single point which would be 'true in itself'."[270] About the truth-seeker, he says, "He forgets that the original perceptual metaphors are metaphors and takes them to be the things themselves."[271] Such statements can easily be taken to assume a metaphysical correspondence theory of truth as Clark believes.

Clark's reading, however, ignores the overall aim of the essay which is to encourage the individual to engage in concept creation. Despite occasional incautious comments, Nietzsche is consistent in insisting that concepts are a human creation that do not reflect the structure of the world. Nietzsche insists "nature is acquainted with no forms and no concepts...[272] Developing the idea that each people has its own conceptual system, Nietzsche says:

> Here one may certainly admire man as a mighty genius of construction, who succeeds in piling up an infinitely complicated dome of concepts upon an unstable foundation, and, as it were, on running water.[273]

---

[269]Nietzsche (1979), 83.
[270]Nietzsche (1979), 85.
[271]Nietzsche (1979), 86.
[272]Nietzsche (1979), 83.
[273]Nietzsche (1979), 85.

In the same vein, Nietzsche says regarding the laws and regularities identified by science, "All that conformity to law, which impresses us so much in the movement of the stars and in chemical processes, coincides at bottom with those properties which we bring to things."[274] Our concepts reflect the creative power of humans not the structure of the world. Nietzsche's point, then, is that the view of language as an instrument of science and its metaphysical correspondence view of truth is incorrect. Instead of assuming such a theory, as Clark argues, Nietzsche is trying to shake us of this standard.

Clark's defense of Nietzsche, then, begins with a misinterpretation of his views as presented in *On Truth and Lies in a Nonmoral Sense*. The reading presented there depends not on a rejection of truth, as she and Danto suggest, but rather on a particular view of the nature of language. Clark may, nonetheless, be correct about Nietzsche's later views. The later Nietzsche may be a neo-Kantian. Clark points to his advocacy of science and common sense as evidence for this neo-Kantianism. She even goes so far as to suggest that Nietzsche lauded science and common sense for avoiding the metaphysical mistakes of philosophy.[275] I will suggest that this, again, gets Nietzsche wrong. Rather, the view of language Nietzsche presents in *On Truth and Lies in a Nonmoral Sense* remains more or less intact throughout the rest of his work.

The later Nietzsche is highly critical of science. Moreover, his criticism of science is the same as his criticism of philosophy. They both embody the ascetic will to truth.[276] Against scientists' insistence that their empirical rationality makes them "free spirits," Nietzsche insists scientists "are far from being *free* spirits: *for*

---

[274]Nietzsche (1979), 88.
[275]Clark (1990), 108.
[276]Nietzsche (1992b), 539-552, 583-592.

*they still have faith in truth.*"[277] Indeed, the task of the scientist assumes the same metaphysical foundations as that of the philosopher:

> That which *constrains* these men [scientists], however, this unconditional will to truth, is *faith in the ascetic ideal itself*...it is the faith in a *metaphysical* value, the absolute value of *truth*, sanctioned and guaranteed by this ideal alone.[278]

Far from neglecting the topic of truth after *Beyond Good & Evil*, as Clark claims, Nietzsche here criticizes scientists for their faith in truth. Indeed, he suggests that the death of God means we have to rethink the will to truth.[279] Instead of science, he believes we should look to art as an ideal and source of meaning.[280] This parallels his encouragement of the intuitive man at the end of *On Truth and Lies in a Nonmoral Sense*.

The later Nietzsche, then, is not uncritical of science. Far from it. However, he does frequently insist that we trust the evidence of our senses. In one epigram in *Beyond Good & Evil* Nietzsche writes, "All credibility, all good conscience, all evidence of truth come only from the senses."[281] This positive assessment of the senses is reprised in *The Anti-Christ*. Speaking of the Christian-Enlightenment view of human nature, he says, " 'Pure spirit' is pure stupidity: if we deduct the nervous system and the senses, the 'mortal frame', *we miscalculate*—that's all!"[282] Nietzsche's advocacy of the senses might seem to indicate advocacy of common sense and science. This may be what Clark is referring to when she insists he advocates science.

---

[277]Nietzsche (1992b), 586.
[278]Nietzsche (1992b), 589.
[279]Nietzsche (1992b), 589.
[280]Nietzsche (1992b), 589-590. The astute reader might recognize the similarity here with Wittgenstein's thought circa the *Tractatus Logico-Philosophicus*.
[281]Nietzsche (1992a), 278.
[282]Nietzsche (1968a), 125.

However, Nietzsche's exhortations of the senses are meant to bring to our attention the varied, disorderly, changing nature of reality. Further, the textual evidence suggests that this view is a constant throughout Nietzsche's thought. Speaking of the faith of philosophers in a "real" world in *Twilight of the Idols*, Nietzsche says, "It is what we *make* of their [the senses'] evidence that first introduces a lie into it, for example, the lie of unity, the lie of materiality, of substance, of duration... 'Reason' is the cause of our falsification of the evidence of the senses."[283] We find similar comments in *Beyond Good & Evil*.[284] Likewise, Nietzsche characterizes Platonism as arising from "*resistence* to obvious sense evidence... the motley whirl of the senses."[285] In *Thus Spoke Zarathustra* he has Zarathustra reflect, "When water is planked over so that it can be walked upon, when gangway and railings span the stream: truly he is not believed who says: 'Everything is in flux.' "[286] Nietzsche's profession of admiration for Heraclitus in *Twilight of the Idols* is due to Heraclitus' recognition of this flux.

The varied, disorderly, changing nature of reality is meant to show us the inadequacy of any single conceptual system. This is particularly aimed against Christian morality. The difficulty facing any critique of Christianity, he observes, is that:

> Out of this erroneous perspective on all things one makes a morality, a virtue, a holiness for oneself, one unites the good conscience with seeing *falsely*—one demands that no *other* perspective shall be accorded any value after one has rendered one's own sacrosanct with the names 'God',

---

[283]Nietzsche (1968b), 36, Cf. Nietzsche (1969), 235-236. Despite her claim that the falsification thesis is absent from Nietzsche's work post-*Beyond Good & Evil*, Clark actually refers to this passage. She argues that the falsification here is confined to philosophers, as opposed to scientists and the ordinary man and, thus, that this passage does not provide evidence against her neo-Kantian reading. For an argument against this claim, the reader is directed to two paragraphs above.

[284]Nietzsche (1992a), 235-237.

[285]Nietzsche (1992a), 212.

[286]Nietzsche (1969), 218.

'redemption', 'eternity'.[287]

Christianity rejects any counter-evidence as illegitimate and inviable. Its putative supernatural foundations are inaccessible to the senses and, thus, invulnerable to any possible counter-evidence. This same problem is present in the putative metaphysical foundations of philosophy and science. If we recognize our nature as bodied beings, however, and turn our attention to the "motley whirl of the senses," Nietzsche hopes we will recognize the absurdity of the claim that any one conceptual system equals ultimate truth. The relationship between the world and our concepts, Nietzsche insists, isn't like that.

Our conceptual systems are particular interpretations of the varied, disorderly, changing nature of reality. These interpretations impose form and order upon reality. The activity of giving form and order is a manifestation of "will to power," which is, he believes, the fundamental drive of life.[288] Nietzsche focuses on the moral because he thinks this aspect of our cultural valuations is particularly pernicious. There is, he has Zarathustra say in *Thus Spoke Zarathustra*, "no greater power on earth than good and evil."[289] However, it is clear that he believes our other concepts are equally the result of human interpretations. On this subject, he says:

> It is *we* alone who have devised cause, sequence, for-each-other, relativity, constraint, number, law, freedom, motive, and purpose; and when we project and mix this symbol world into things as it if existed 'in itself,' we act once more as we have always acted—*mythologically.*[290]

The concepts enumerated are from the sciences, mathematics, morality, and politics. These concepts form a system which we project upon the world, giving it form, just

---

[287]Nietzsche (1968a), 120. This is yet another post-*Beyond Good & Evil* passage in which Clark's falsification thesis appears.

[288]Cf. Nietzsche (1992a), 393, Nietzsche (1992b), 515.

[289]Nietzsche (1969), 84.

[290]Nietzsche (1992a), 219.

as via our interpretations of our physio-psychological experience and characteristics give form to ourselves. Our concepts, in Nietzschean terms, are a manifestation of our will to power.

Overcoming, then, is the process of creating and applying concepts. Consider the following passage in which Nietzsche discusses the Platonic origins of Christian morality:

> ...the charm of the Platonic way of thinking, which was a *noble* way of thinking, consisted precisely in *resistance* to obvious sense-evidence...and by means of pale, cold, gray concept nets which they threw over the motley whirl of the senses...In this overcoming of the world, and interpreting the world in the manner of Plato, there was an *enjoyment* different from that which the physicists offer us today...[291]

We overcome the varied, disorderly, changing nature of reality by giving it form and order through the application of concepts to it. Similarly, we overcome ourselves by creating and applying concepts to the unorganized chaos of our instincts.

Nietzsche's view of language provides a coherent, non-metaphorical account of overcoming. Overcoming is the process of giving form and order to the variable, disordered, changing nature of reality by creating and applying concepts. Self-overcoming is this process applied to the chaos of our instincts. Additionally, this view of language works to free the Nietzschean individual from the moral sanctions of modernity. The Nietzschean individual, realizing she is unconstrained by any one interpretation, sees that she is able to revise, create, and apply concepts of her own. She is able to revise the interpretation she was given and, thereby, to carry out Nietzsche's hoped-for cultural revival.

The Nietzschean individual provides a model for our individual caught in a moment of culture crisis. Recall, the problem facing our individual is that the

---

[291]Nietzsche (1992a), 212.

world-picture of her culture no longer helps her make sense of the world in which she finds herself. In particular, her idea of the good life is no longer practically realizable. As such, it is no longer helpful in guiding her decisions and is, rather, a source of delusion or disappointment. In order to avoid an unfulfilling fate, she must find a way to escape or change her world-picture and the expectations it gives her. That is, she must, like the Nietzschean individual, recognize her creative nature and revise, create, and apply concepts of her own. The solution to the problem of culture crisis, then, rests in the process of overcoming. The solution lies in creating a new interpretation of ourselves and the world.

Against Clark's neo-Kantian defense of Nietzsche, I suggested that Nietzsche embraces a particular view of language. I argued that Nietzsche rejects a metaphysical correspondence theory of truth as a consequence of this view. His alternate view of language gives a coherent and non-metaphorical account of the process of overcoming. As such, this view of language is essential to Nietzsche's project, the Nietzschean individual, and the fate of our individual caught in a moment of culture crisis.

## VITAMIN W

Though Nietzsche wrote extended passages on the nature of language and its relationship to culture, he did not produce a full-fledged philosophy of language. Indeed, though we can get a general sense of his view of language, his ideas remain underdeveloped. Further, though he was an excellent culture critic, Nietzsche was not a very careful philosopher of language. This carelessness has left him open to criticism from more persnickety philosophers. But this view of the nature of language is essential to a non-metaphorical understanding of overcoming.

Though Nietzsche leaves his view of language severely underdeveloped, we can get a sense of his thoughts on the subject. The central insight of this view is that we give order and form to ourselves and the world via the creation and application of concepts. Nietzsche's other insights are dependent upon this one. We are creative animals because we create ourselves and the world via our conceptual interpretations. There are no metaphysical or supernatural truths because these assume an enduring source of truth prior and external to our interpretations. Nietzsche calls on the Nietzschean individual to resolve the problems of modernity by engaging in overcoming and, thereby, carrying out a cultural revival. This solution is only coherent given his view of language.

Though we can get a sense of Nietzsche's thoughts about the nature of language, the sketchiness of his views is problematic. Moreover, his blustering, often incautious style is ill-suited to the delicate task of language philosophy. We can see the results of such incaution in Clark's response to Nietzsche's view of language as metaphor. Metaphor, she argues, requires a conceptual counterpart and thus, not all language can be metaphor.[292] Danto has a similar objection to Nietzsche's creative or imaginative uses of concepts in art. Such imaginative uses, he argues, must have ordinary counterparts.[293] Such non-metaphorical or ordinary uses of language or concepts, they insist, must be the correct use. These objections misunderstand Nietzsche's point.

Rather than leaving Nietzsche to his own devices on the topic of language, I suggest we look to Wittgenstein for supplementary treatment on the subject. Wittgenstein's view on the nature of language shares Nietzsche's central insight that language is a system of concepts by which we give form and order to the world.

[292]Clark (1990), 69-77.
[293]Danto (2005), 26-28.

Moreover, Wittgenstein is much more careful than Nietzsche and gave the topic of language a more comprehensive treatment. This allows us to flesh out Nietzsche's insights in Wittgensteinian terms. According to this suggestion, we should think of Nietzsche's view of language in terms of a Wittgensteinian language-game. In Wittgensteinian terms, then, overcoming is a process of revising or creating the world-picture and concepts of our language.

Wittgenstein can help us make sense of Nietzsche. But the favor goes both ways. Whereas Nietzsche was not a particularly skilled language philosopher, Wittgenstein was not a very good culture critic.[294] The comparison with Nietzsche gives a plausible explanation as to the connection von Wright says Wittgenstein saw between his thought and "features of our culture or civilization."[295] The suggestion is that Wittgenstein saw that his view of language is essential to understanding culture and our world-picture as a human creation, subject to human revision and creation. In articulating his view of language Wittgenstein hoped to show us that the cultural problems from which he saw us suffering were within our power to resolve. By articulating his view of language, he hoped to reorient our understanding of the relationship between ourselves, language, and the world and, thereby, show us the way out of the fly-bottle we have constructed for ourselves.[296]

The resonances between these two thinkers have not gone unnoticed. Erich Heller first compared them in a 1966 essay. Heller argued that the intellectual development of Nietzsche and Wittgenstein followed a similar arc. The thought of both men, he says, is characterized by the rejection of metaphysics and "the loss of faith in any pre-established correspondence between, on the one hand, the logic of

---

[294]Consider the complete absence of the notion of power in Wittgenstein. Cf. Sluga (2011), 128-129.
[295]von Wright (1998), 110.
[296]Wittgenstein (1967), §309.

our thought and language, and, on the other hand, the 'logic' of Reality."[297] Heller thinks the turn to language by both thinkers is a mistake which signals the end of good, productive philosophy.[298]

Gordon Bearn develops a more optimistic version of this comparison in his 1997 work *Waking to Wonder* in which he argues that linguistic meaning and existential meaning are inextricably bound up with one another.[299] Many other commentators have compared Nietzsche and Wittgenstein in passing, including von Wright, Pippin, Pitkin, Robinson, and Sluga.[300]

David Owen has developed this comparison in a different direction. Both thinkers, he argues, help us understand the phenomenon of what he refers to as "aspectival captivity." Aspectival captivity is a kind of non-physical captivity different in kind from ideological captivity.[301] The aspect that holds us captive is a particular picture or perspective of the world that we inherit pre-rationally and which underlies our judgments and beliefs.[302] The problem of aspectival captivity is that sometimes our picture or perspective stops being helpful.[303] At times, he says:

> ... given changes in the conditions of worldly activity, we may come to experience our world picture or some aspect of it as problematic in that we are increasingly unable to make sense of ourselves as agents in this way. In other words, a disjuncture may emerge between our ways of making sense of ourselves, on the one hand, and our cares and commitments, on the other.[304]

When our picture or perspective no longer helps us in making sense of ourselves and

[297]Heller (1976), 214.
[298]Heller (1976), 225-226.
[299]Cf. Sontag (1995) for a further exploration of the existential and mystical in Wittgenstein.
[300]von Wright (1998), 115, Pippin (2009), 45, 72, Pitkin (1972), 336, Robinson (2009), 29, 32, 48, 148, Sluga (2011), 15, 76, 82-86.
[301]Owen (2003), 84.
[302]Owen (2003), 84, 89.
[303]Owen (2003), 89.
[304]Owen (2003), 84.

our lives, we need a way to "call [it] into question in order to assess its *value*."[305]

As aspectival captivity concerns pre-rationally accepted pictures or perspectives of the world, it requires a different kind of critique from ideological captivity. Owen refers to this kind of critique as "aspectival therapy" and argues that Wittgenstein's perspicuous representation and Nietzsche's genealogy are two forms.[306] These methods reorient "our relationship to our current ways of thinking."[307] They put on display the problematic disjuncture between "our ways of making sense of ourselves and our cares and commitments" and show us the possibility of other pictures or perspectives.[308]

This comparison is helpful in understanding each thinker's respective project. Both thinkers were concerned with the state of culture in their respective eras. Additionally, both saw that the tenacity of this cultural problem was due to a certain misleading understanding of the relationship between ourselves, language, and the world. Nietzsche employed his talent to articulate the problem of culture and identified overcoming as the solution. Wittgenstein employed his talent to explore the nature of language and saw that something like his view of language was necessary in order to make sense of this cultural problem and its solution.

This chapter was concerned with Nietzsche's view of language. It was suggested that this view of language is essential to giving a coherent, non-metaphorical account of overcoming which is central to Nietzsche's project. Given this non-metaphorical account of overcoming, the Nietzschean individual provides a model

---

[305]Owen (2003), 85.
[306]Owen (2003), 82.
[307]Owen (2003), 87.
[308]Owen (2003), 86-87. Cf. Owen (2001), Owen (2002).

for our individual caught in a moment of culture crisis. As this view of language is importantly similar to Wittgenstein's, it was suggested that we think of Nietzsche's insights in Wittgensteinian terms. Moreover, this comparison provides a highly plausible explanation as to the connection Wittgenstein saw between his views and the human condition.

However, some commentators argue that Wittgenstein's view of language renders the individual incapable of concept revision, creation, and application. Thus, the appeal to a Wittgensteinian view of language may preclude the Nietzschean individual. That is, Wittgenstein may simply give us reason to be dissatisfied with our beliefs and judgments, via his perspicuous representation, without giving us a way to change them. This would leave our individual caught in a moment of culture crisis in the lurch, if you will. The next chapter will consider the relationship between the individual and language in Wittgenstein's thought.

# WITTGENSTEIN ON TALKING TO YOURSELF

The resonances between Nietzsche's and Wittgenstein's thought have not gone completely unnoticed. Nonetheless, the assertion that there are important similarities and sympathies between these thinkers is often met with incredulity. Bearn noted such a response in his 1997 *Waking to Wonder* despite the fact that his work elaborated on Heller's work which first appeared over thirty years prior.[309] Such incredulity has also characterized this author's own experience. The source of this incredulity is likely due to significant dissonances in interpretation. As we saw in the second chapter, commentators have often taken Wittgenstein's work on the nature of language to have conservative implications. On the other hand, Nietzsche is often taken to be highly radical.

The suggestion of the previous chapter is that the differences between Nietzsche and Wittgenstein are not so significant. While they focused on different aspects, Nietzsche and Wittgenstein are concerned with the same problem. They are concerned with the phenomenon of cultural decline, its sources, symptoms, and solution. Both thinkers appeal to the individual, trying to shake her free of the picture or perspective that holds her captive. Nietzsche calls upon the Nietzschean individual to carry out a cultural revival. Wittgenstein explores the nature of language showing that such a project is even coherent. This chapter will consider the challenge that an appeal to a Wittgensteinian view of language precludes the Nietzschean individual.

---

[309]Bearn (1997), 79.

# ANTI-INDIVIDUALIST READINGS

I argued in the third chapter that the Nietzschean individual is only possible if the notion of overcoming is coherent. I suggested in the fourth chapter that the notion of overcoming is dependent on Nietzsche's view of language. This view of language shares its key insight with Wittgenstein's view of language. As such, I suggested that we can look to Wittgenstein's view of language to flesh out Nietzsche's views. However, several commentators have interpreted Wittgenstein as forwarding a collectivist or communitarian account of meaning. If these commentators are correct, this view of language will only serve to preclude the Nietzschean individual. This section will provide an examination of the relevant commentary.

It will be helpful to introduce two characters. Crusoe and life-long Crusoe are recurring characters in the debate as to whether Wittgenstein's view of language is individualist or anti-individualist. "Crusoe" is a character borrowed from Robert Louis Stevenson's novel who became stranded on an island as an adult. For our purposes, the importance of Crusoe is that he is a physically isolated, competent speaker of his native language. He engages in one- and two-person language-games, playing both roles where necessary. He is important insofar as his conceptual possibility undercuts the idea that meaningful use of language requires a physically present linguistic community. "Life-long Crusoe" is a twist on the Crusoe character who is physically and socially isolated and a competent speaker of some language of his own invention. He is important insofar as his conceptual possibility undercuts the idea that language is essentially social insofar as the existence of language requires a linguistic community.

The debate centered on these characters does not directly speak to our concern for the Nietzschean individual. The Nietzschean individual is neither a Crusoe nor life-long Crusoe. She does not, like Crusoe, simply continue to use language as it was given her. She creates new concepts and new language-games. Unlike the life-long Crusoe, the Nietzschean individual is taught a language in the normal way. Each of the following readings of Wittgenstein will have to be assessed individually as to their verdict on each of these characters. Some fairly interesting combinations are in evidence.

As we saw in the second chapter, Georg von Wright notes that Wittgenstein saw a connection between his thought and the human condition. It is clear, says von Wright, that Wittgenstein saw a connection between "features of our culture and civilization" and language-games.[310] According to von Wright's Wittgenstein, problems in our culture or civilization manifest as "a distortion or malfunction of the language-games."[311] The problems of philosophy are symptoms of problems in our culture.[312] Resolution of these distortions or malfunctions will involve resolution of a corresponding problem with the way we live.[313] Von Wright insists, however, that while Wittgenstein saw a connection between his thought and the human condition, he "certainly did not think this [the resolution of such cultural problems was] possible through the efforts of an individual."[314]

The conclusion that the individual is powerless to address our cultural problems follows from von Wright's communitarian interpretation of Wittgenstein's view of language. According to Wittgenstein, he says, the individual is "deeply entrenched in basic structures of a *social* nature."[315] That is, the individual's world-picture, which is the background of her beliefs and judgments, is given to her by society.

---

[310]von Wright (1998), 110.
[311]von Wright (1998), 111.
[312]von Wright (1998), 112.
[313]von Wright (1998), 111.
[314]von Wright (1998), 113.
[315]von Wright (1998), 111.

Von Wright says, for Wittgenstein "the individual's beliefs, judgments, and thought are entrenched in unquestionably accepted language-games and socially sanctioned forms of life."[316] This unquestioning acceptance forms the basis of meaningful language. The attempt to take a critical stance towards our language-games and forms of life would undermine the individual's very ability to make judgments, form beliefs, or perform actions. On von Wright's reading, Wittgenstein's view of language precludes life-long Crusoe and the Nietzschean individual.

Perhaps the most famous collectivist reading of Wittgenstein is Kripke's as presented in his 1982 *Wittgenstein on Rules and Private Language*. This collectivist reading turns on an interpretation of the private language argument. Kripke takes the private language argument to be concerned with the problem of following a rule.[317] Kripke glosses Wittgenstein's claim that rules fix meaning to mean that meaning is fixed by consistent usage of a word through time.[318] The problem, Kripke argues, is that there is no fact about the individual that determines that her present usage conforms to her previous usage.[319] According to this reading, the individual's "finite mind" is not capable of establishing meaning.[320] To resolve this problem, which Kripke characterizes as a kind of scepticism regarding meaning, we must turn to collectively determined assertability conditions.[321] It is only because we "generally agree" about the meaning of a word that language is possible at all.[322] Without

---

[316] von Wright (1998), 118.

[317] Kripke (1982), vii, 2-3, 45. Kripke thinks rule-following must be the focus of the private language argument because the ability of an individual to identify her own sensations seems obviously unproblematic to him. "How can," Kripke asks, "I possibly have any difficulty identifying my own sensations? And if there were a difficulty, how could 'public' criteria help me?" Kripke (1982), 62 This is a puzzling gloss of the argument that reappears fairly frequently. Cf. Pears (1988), 328, Rundle (2009), 138, 151, Sluga (2011), 73.

[318] Kripke (1982), 40.

[319] Cf. Kripke (1982), 11-14.

[320] Kripke (1982), 21, 54, 69, 89.

[321] Kripke (1982), 74, 79.

[322] Kripke (1982), 97.

"reference to a community," Kripke maintains, words cannot have any determinate meaning.[323] This reading excludes Crusoe, life-long Crusoe, and the Nietzschean individual.

David Bloor develops Kripke's collectivist reading. Like Kripke, the idea of rule-following serves as the crux of Bloor's collectivist reading. On a Wittgensteinian view of language, for a word to be meaningful there must be "a real difference between its being applied correctly and its being applied in correctly."[324] As such, Bloor claims, meaning is intimately connected with the notion of rule-following, or the normativity of rules. If we look to how we learn rules, as Wittgenstein suggests, a collectivist view of language emerges.[325] Bloor argues that Wittgenstein forwarded a finitist theory of meaning according to which we create and expand meaning every time we apply the rule to a new case.[326] In applying rules to new cases we are guided by "our instinctive (but socially educated) sense of 'sameness'."[327] Our words are meaningful, then, because collective consensus guides our application of rules and, thereby, provides the normativity needed for rule-following.[328] The individual, as the private language argument suggests, cannot create this normativity for herself.[329] It isn't clear that Bloor's view excludes Crusoe, but his collectivist view of meaning precludes life-long Crusoe and the Nietzschean individual.

Norman Malcolm continues the theme of community agreement. Malcolm rejects Kripke's characterization of Wittgenstein as a sceptic regarding meaning, but his argument is similar to Bloor's in that he argues that the concept of rule-following

---

[323]Kripke (1982), 79, Cf. Kripke (1982), 88, 89.
[324]Bloor (2004), 117.
[325]Bloor (1983), 9.
[326]Bloor (1983), 9-19, 136.
[327]Bloor (1983), 17.
[328]Bloor (1983), 17.
[329]Bloor (1983), 55, 69, Cf. Bloor (2004), 117, 118.

requires a community.[330] A rule, on Malcolm's reading, is a *communal* practice, custom, or institution.[331] In order to follow a rule, there must be agreement as to what a rule means and requires.[332] Such agreement is necessary, says Malcolm, for the existence of language at all:

> ... Wittgenstein is saying, clearly enough, that *without* general agreement as to what is 'the same', as to whether going on *thus* fits *this* rule—there would not be rules, descriptions, or language, but at most 'a confusion of tongues'.[333]

This is very similar to Bloor's argument from meaning finitism. The individual's finite mind, intentions, and actions are not sufficient to establish a rule. Rather, general agreement is required. This agreement, Malcolm argues, is "exhibited in uniformity of behavior," that is, in many people taking part in the same form of life.[334] The socially determined rule fixes the ordinary use of a word and thereby constitutes the standard of correct use.[335]

Malcolm's gloss on the private language argument follows from this communitarian reading of Wittgenstein's view of language. General agreement is required for meaning. Malcolm argues that because the objects of the private language are essentially private there can be no general consensus as to the application of the names of the private language. Without this basis for distinguishing between correct and incorrect application of a rule, there can be no meaningful private language.[336]

---

[330]Malcolm (1988), 154-155, Malcolm (1989), 6.
[331]Malcolm (1988), 156.
[332]Malcolm (1989), 13.
[333]Malcolm (1989), 10.
[334]Malcolm (1989), 13, 22, 25.
[335]Cf. Malcolm (1981).
[336]Malcolm (1988), 158-159.

Malcolm finds the possibility of a Crusoe obvious and uninteresting, but his communitarian reading leads him to reject the life-long Crusoe.[337] This communitarian reading precludes the Nietzschean individual as well.

John Canfield forwards a view similar to Malcolm's. Like Malcolm, Canfield takes rule-following to require a community.[338] He takes it to be the case that a linguistic community consists of at least two speakers and is characterized by two-person language-games. This view takes for granted that communication is the function of language.[339] However, Canfield argues that Wittgenstein takes language to be a family resemblance concept. Thus, while two-person language-games are our paradigmatic example of language, he believes that Wittgenstein allows for a language characterized by one-person language-games, such as Wittgenstein's monologuists.[340] Canfield argues that, as things stand, our concept of language is able to be analogically extended to these non-paradigmatic cases.[341] However, such analogical extension is not possible in the case of putative private languages.[342] Private language, Canfield says, is too different from other cases of language for the concept to apply.[343] Despite his collectivist reading, Canfield's view can accommodate Crusoe, life-long Crusoe, and the Nietzschean individual given an analogical extension

[337]Malcolm (1988), 5, 25.

[338]Canfield (1996), 470.

[339]Canfield (1996), 474-477.

[340]Canfield (1996), 478. Canfield introduces "Simple Crusoe" and "Sophisticated Crusoe" to mediate between Malcolm and Hacker and Baker, who introduce an individualist reading of Wittgenstein which we will see later. The Simple Crusoe "masters" only one-person language-games but may have the ability to learn two-person language-games. The Sophisticated Crusoe "masters" both one-person and some two-person language-games. Canfield (1996), 480. It's not clear, however, that these characters line up with the Crusoe and life-long Crusoe we met earlier. Both of his Crusoes seem to be socially and physically isolated from the start and the question appears to be whether they can develop language as communication with others, taking for granted that they will be able to play language-games with themselves. The debate Canfield sees, then, is very different from the debate in which other commentators are engaged.

[341]Canfield (1996), 478, 480-481, 484, 485.

[342]Canfield (1996), 485, 486.

[343]Canfield (1996), 486.

of our concept of language.

Stewart Candlish provides a different kind of reading of the private language argument. Candlish argues that the private language argument has the form of a reductio.[344] The crux of the argument is the notion of private ostensive definition.[345] The private linguist takes it to be the case that the individual can assign meaning to a sensation word by fixing her attention upon a sensation and uttering a word. The problem, Candlish argues, is that this account makes no distinction between meaning and naming. It treats the thing named as the meaning of the word. But this means that we can only correctly use this sensation word in the presence of the named sensation.[346] That is, private ostensive definition is insufficient to establish a rule for using the word and is, therefore, insufficient to establish meaning.[347] What we need to secure meaning, says Candlish, is to turn to some publically accessible phenomenon.[348] However, while Candlish argues that private ostensive definition is insufficient to establish meaning, he does not follow Kripke, Bloor, and Malcolm in concluding that meaning requires a community of speakers. Candlish's reading of the private language argument, then, leaves the question of Crusoe, life-long Crusoe, and the Nietzschean individual untouched.

Peter Hacker and Gordon Baker forward an individualist reading of the private language argument. They agree with Candlish that the private language argument

[344]Candlish (1980), 87.

[345]Candlish (1980), 87-88, 91.

[346]Candlish (1980), 90.

[347]Candlish (1980), 91.

[348]Candlish (1980), 92, Cf. Pears (1988). Pears offers a weaker version of this reading according to which public objects and other speakers act as external constants that we look to as "checks" on our usage rather than necessary elements of language. Pears (1988), 368. Additionally, rather than taking private language to be incoherent, Pears takes Wittgenstein to argue that our ability to create and maintain a sensation language depends on our first having a physical object language. Pears (1988), 357. However, Pears attributes an unarticulated premise to Wittgenstein which assumes an Augustinian view of language and indicates that Pears missed the point. Pears (1988), 414.

rests on the incoherence of private ostensive definition.[349] However, Hacker and Baker go on to make explicit that they do not believe this implies that meaning requires a community of speakers. What the private language argument shows, they argue, is that the rules of a language must be shareable.[350] But, contra Kripke, Bloor and Malcolm, this does not mean that a language must be shared.[351] Hacker and Baker reject the claim that communal agreement as to what the rule means and requires is needed. Following a rule, Hacker and Baker explain, is simply a regularity of behavior—a practice; part of a way of life.[352] Such practices require only a "multiplicity of occasions" rather than a "multiplicity of agents," as the collectivist and communitarian readings hold.[353] What a rule means and requires is determined by the rule itself.[354] The individual, Hacker and Baker insist, can perfectly well use concepts and even a whole language of her own innovation.[355] On Hacker's and Baker's view, Crusoe, life-long Crusoe, and the Nietzschean individual are all unquestionably conceptually possible.

My concern for the Nietzschean individual predisposes me to favor an individualist reading like Hacker's and Baker's. Nonetheless, I am sympathetic when Malcolm says he is "dissatisfied... with the lack of importance they [Hacker and Baker] assign to the presence of a community..."[356] Hacker goes so far as to dismiss the idea of "form of life" as wholly unimportant to Wittgenstein's thought.[357] But

---

[349]Baker and Hacker (1984), 14, 23. Cf. Baker and Hacker (1990), 179, Hacker (2010), 100.

[350]Baker and Hacker (1990), 168.

[351]Baker and Hacker (1990), 171.

[352]Hacker (2010), 93-96, Baker and Hacker (1984), 53.

[353]Hacker (2010), 97.

[354]Baker and Hacker (1984), 72. Baker and Hacker argue that the communitarian and collectivist readings of the private language argument assume that we need an external standard to provide a basis for something like objective truth. They suggest that this just assumes an Augustinian view of language. Baker and Hacker (1984), 75, 95, 116, 119.

[355]Hacker (2010), 105, 108-109, Baker and Hacker (1990), 172.

[356]Malcolm (1989), 5.

[357]From conversation.

the dispute between Malcolm and Hacker and Baker assumes that the choice is between a communitarian or an individualist reading. That is, they assume that either the individual is inescapably embedded in an essentially social language or that the community plays no important role and the individual is free to do whatever she wants, linguistically speaking. Neither of these positions seems to me to capture the relationship Wittgenstein sees between the individual, community, and language.

As the above survey suggests, the possibility of the Nietzschean individual depends upon whether language on Wittgenstein's view is essentially social. As evidence, collectivist and communitarian commentators point to rules and the private language argument. The next section will provide an alternate reading of these aspects of Wittgenstein's thought. Against collectivist and communitarian readings, it will be argued that something like Hacker's and Baker's view is correct. However, it will also be argued against Hacker and Baker that Wittgenstein believed that the linguistic community plays an important role with regard to language and the individual. The following reading, thereby, aims to transcend the communitarian-individualist debate.

## RULES AND PRIVATE LANGUAGE

Anti-individualist readings of Wittgenstein take his investigation of rules and private language as evidence that language is essentially social. They argue that rules require collective agreement or a community of speakers. As meaning is fixed by rules, meaning is impossible without a linguistic community. They point to the private language argument as further evidence. The individual, they argue, is like Wittgenstein's diarist. Her actions are insufficient to establish meaning, just as the diarist's actions are insufficient to establish meaning for her sensation words. Therefore, they conclude, language is essentially social. In this section I will argue that anti-individualist readings misunderstand Wittgenstein on rules and private language.

In the Preface to his *Philosophical Investigations*, Wittgenstein offers some disparaging comments regarding the work. "I should have liked," he says, "to produce a good book. This has not come about, but the time is past in which I could improve it."[358] Despite his own hesitancies, the first half of the first part of the *Philosophical Investigations* represents a clear and concerted attack on the Augustinian view of language and a development of his own alternative view.[359]

Wittgenstein presents the Augustinian view in the first remark quoting Augustine's description of his experience learning language:

> When they (my elders) named some object, and accordingly moved towards something, I saw this and I grasped that the thing was called by the sound they uttered when they meant to point it out. Their intention was shewn by their bodily movements, as it were the natural language of all peoples: the expression of the face, the play of the eyes, the movement of other parts of the body, and the tone of voice which expresses our state of mind in seeking, having, rejecting, or avoiding something. Thus, as I heard words repeatedly used in their proper places in various sentences, I gradually learnt to understand what objects they signified; and after I had trained my mouth to form these signs, I used them to express my own desires. [360]

This description takes for granted a particular view of the nature of language. It assumes that the world is divided into various kinds of objects and that words are like names. Sentences assert propositions about states of affairs and are true or

---

[358]Wittgenstein (1967), x.

[359]I say the first half of the first part because it seems to me that Wittgenstein's argument loses some of its clarity after the private language argument, not because he stops attacking the Augustianian view.

[360]Wittgenstein (1967), 2 fn.

false insofar as they correctly represent these. It assumes that we learn language via ostensive definition whereby an object is indicated and a word is uttered. Further, it assumes that understanding meaning is a mental process of getting the connection between words and their referents correct.[361]

Wittgenstein's alternate language-game picture of the nature of language brings the question of rules to the forefront. Against the Augustinian view, he argues, the meaning of a word is not the object to which it refers. Rather, the meaning of a word is fixed by its role in the language-game. That is, the meaning of a word is determined by the rules that govern the various things we do with it. The meaning of a word is fixed by the rules for its use.

However, these rules are not like the axioms of a calculus. The various uses of a word are not all determined beforehand by the rule.[362] The rule is indefinite. But the indefinite nature of rules, Wittgenstein argues, does not mean that the meaning of the word is indeterminate.[363] To bring out this point, Wittgenstein likens indefinite rules to infinite series. The members of a series cannot all be given beforehand precisely because there are an infinite number of them. However, if we understand the function, then given any particular input we can give the correct output.[364] Similarly, an indefinite rule, despite being indefinite, is able to fix meaning in normal circumstances.[365]

The indefinite nature of these rules opens Wittgenstein to a Kripkean objection. If the application of the rule, says the objector, is not determined beforehand, then the rule is open to an infinite number of interpretations. But this just means

---

[361]The perceptive reader will be reminded of Russell's view of language.
[362]Wittgenstein (1958), 25, Wittgenstein (1967), §§97-107.
[363]Wittgenstein (1967), §§68-71, §§79-88.
[364]Wittgenstein (1967), §§148-155, §§179-197.
[365]Wittgenstein (1967), §142.

that the rule which is meant to fix the meaning of the word doesn't fix anything at all.[366] Wittgenstein summarizes this objection when he says:

> This was our paradox: no course of action could be determined by a rule because every course of action can be made out to accord with the rule. The answer was: if everything can be made out to accord with the rule, then it can also be made out to conflict with it. And so there could be neither accord nor conflict here.[367]

Wittgenstein suggests, however, that this objection shows that a mistake has been made. There must, he says, be a "way of grasping a rule which is *not* an *interpretation*."[368] Understanding a word is not a matter of interpreting a rule, but rather of "obeying the rule."[369] That is, understanding a word is not a mental process, but a practice, an activity, a way of behaving.[370]

At the time of the *Philosophical Investigations*, Wittgenstein has some trouble explaining the idea of acting in accordance with a rule without interpretation. He likens rules to orders and says that we are trained to obey them. We react in particular ways.[371] He says:

> If I have exhausted the justification I have reached bedrock, and my spade is turned. Then I am inclined to say: "This is simply what I do."[372]

Similarly, after suggesting we think of rules as symbolic formulas, Wittgenstein explains:

---

[366]Wittgenstein (1967), §198.
[367]Wittgenstein (1967), §201.
[368]Wittgenstein (1967), §201.
[369]Wittgenstein (1967), §201.
[370]Wittgenstein (1967), §202.
[371]Wittgenstein (1967), §206.
[372]Wittgenstein (1967), §217.

—I should have said: *This is how it strikes me.*
When I obey a rule, I do not choose.
I obey the rule *blindly*.[373]

Further on, Wittgenstein says:

"But surely you can see...?" That is just the characteristic expression
of someone who is under the compulsion of a rule.[374]

Against anti-individualist readings, rules do not need to be interpreted. Rather, the rule itself tells us what it requires. When we learn a rule we learn a certain way of seeing and doing.

Wittgenstein has trouble explaining what he means here. However, it is clear from the text that he means something like the idea of a world-picture which he introduces later in *On Certainty*. Consider the following passage:

Disputes do not break out (among mathematicians, say) over the question whether a rule has been obeyed or not. People don't come to blows about it, for example. That is part of the framework on which the working of our language is based (for example, in giving descriptions).[375]

Like our world-picture, these rules shape the unquestioned background against which we form beliefs and make judgments. In learning rules we adopt a particular world-picture that shapes how we see the world and, thereby, how we act in it.

Though our use of words is guided by these rules, applying rules does not require interpretation. Wittgenstein re-articulates this in *On Certainty* when he says, "But the most important thing is: the rule is not needed. Nothing is lacking. We do calculate according to a rule, and that is enough."[376] Rules form the framework

---

[373]Wittgenstein (1967), §219.
[374]Wittgenstein (1967), §231.
[375]Wittgenstein (1967), §240.
[376]Wittgenstein (1969), 46, Cf. 44, 47.

that underlies our language, the world-picture that forms the background of our judgments and beliefs. The bare fact that meaning is fixed by rules, then, does not require collective agreement or a community of speakers to interpret the rules for individuals. By shaping our world-picture, the rules themselves tell us what is required.

Against the anti-individualists, then, rules do not require a collective or community to interpret them. As Hacker and Baker note, the agreement necessary is between cases, not between speakers. However, this does not mean the collective or community plays no role in language nor that it is only agreement between cases that matters for Wittgenstein. Wittgenstein says:

> If language is to be a means of communication there must be agreement not only in definitions but also (queer as this may sound) in judgments.[377]

This is a conditional statement. Insofar as language is a means of communication, we must agree about definitions and judgments. This, again, is a foreshadowing of the notion of a world-picture that Wittgenstein introduces in *On Certainty*. The idea is simply that communication requires that we share a world-picture. In order to communicate we must operate with common background judgments and beliefs.

Communication is a highly important function of language. However, contra Canfield, communication is not the essential function of language. Wittgenstein's monologuists example makes this clear:

> A human being can encourage himself, give himself orders, obey, blame and punish himself; he can ask himself a question and answer it. We could even imagine human beings who spoke only in monologue; who accompanied their activities by talking to themselves.—An explorer who watched

---

[377]Wittgenstein (1967), §242.

them and listened to their talk might succeed in translating their language into ours. (This would enable him to predict these people's actions correctly, for he also hears them making resolutions and decisions.)[378]

Communication, on Wittgenstein's view, requires that we have a common world-picture. But language is not essentially communicative. Not only do individuals use language by themselves, but we can imagine a group of individuals who have only ever spoken to themselves.

The monologuists example tells against anti-individualist readings in another way. Some anti-individualist commentators take the fact that we learn language via social processes to indicate that language is essentially social. Bloor, for instance, takes Wittgenstein's exhortations that we look to how we learn language to lead to his collectivist conclusion.[379] Malcolm complains that Hacker's and Baker's individualistic reading requires that "(miraculously) they [the monologuists] developed the *same* language."[380] This seems miraculous because they did not learn their language from other speakers whereas we do. However, the question of how language is learned is clearly not relevant in the monologuists example. By forwarding this example, Wittgenstein is insisting that the conceptual requirements of language do not preclude this possibility. The fact that we do learn language via social processes does not make social learning a conceptually necessary feature of language.

Anti-individualist commentators are likely to object that I cannot make sense of the private language argument. As we saw above, these commentators take the private language argument to show that the individual is incapable of fixing meaning alone. However, if we compare the monologuists with the private linguist, a different aim emerges. Recall, the monologuists "accompanied their activities by talking to

---

[378]Wittgenstein (1967), §243, cf. §491.
[379]Bloor (1983), 9.
[380]Malcolm (1989), 19.

themselves."[381] On the other hand, in the case of the private linguist, Wittgenstein asks us to suppose that he does not "have any natural expression for the sensation," such as crying is a natural expression of pain.[382] The private linguist is supposed to create a private language by noting his sensations and associating words with them, keeping records as to which words he used in a diary.[383] These sensations are completely dissociated with any activity. The central question of the private language argument, then, is whether there can be a language completely dissociated from activity.[384]

Let's examine the case. The diarist goes through the procedure of private ostensive definition. He focuses his attention on a sensation and utters a word. He is thereby supposed to have given a definition of a sensation word. Wittgenstein objects:

> —But "I impresss it on myself" can only mean: this process brings it about that I remember the connexion *right* in the future. But in the present case I have no criterion of correctness. One would like to say: whatever is going to seem right to me is right. And that only means here that we can't talk about "right".[385]

The objection is that private ostension is not sufficient for creating a rule or technique for using a word. However, the source of the insufficiency is not the absence of a linguistic community, but rather the absence of criteria. The act of private ostension is not sufficient to provide a "criterion of correctness" because, by supposition, there

---

[381]Wittgenstein (1967), §243.
[382]Wittgenstein (1967), §256.
[383]Wittgenstein (1967), §258.
[384]Interestingly, Malcolm takes the private language argument to be centered on the "private activity" of the private linguist. He seems to mean this as opposed to "communal activity." However, this misses the difference between the monologuists and the private linguist. Malcolm (1988), 156-158.
[385]Wittgenstein (1967), §258.

is no activity to play the role of criteria.[386] There is no activity to fix the meaning to his words.[387]

This reading finds support in an elaboration on the topic of criteria a little further on. Wittgenstein says:

> Let us remember that there are certain criteria in a man's behaviour for the fact that he does not understand a word: that it means nothing to him, that he can do nothing with it. And criteria for his "thinking he understands", attaching some meaning to the word, but not the right one. And, lastly, criteria for his undersanding the word right. In the second case one might speak of a subjective understanding. And sounds which no one else understands but which I "*appear to understand*" might be called a "private language".[388]

The criteria for whether a person understands a word is exhibited in his behavior or activity. A person understands a word correctly when he acts in a particular way. According to the parameters of private language, however, there is no behavior or activity to serve as criteria. As such, there is no basis for making a distinction between understanding or not understanding private language. Such a language is no language at all.

As anti-individualist commentators have noted, there is an important connection between Wittgenstein's investigation of rules and private language. Wittgenstein makes this connection in the course of his investigation of rules:

> And hence also "obeying a rule" is a practice. And to *think* one is obeying a rule is not to obey a rule. Hence it is not possible to obey a rule "privately": otherwise thinking one was obeying a rule would be the same thing as obeying it.[389]

---

[386]Cf. Wittgenstein (1967), §580.

[387]In the *Blue and Brown Books* Wittgenstein offers a different but related objection. Cf. Wittgenstein (1958), 73-74, 172.

[388]Wittgenstein (1967), §269.

[389]Wittgenstein (1967), §202.

Kripke and Malcolm have pointed to this passage as indicating that an individual's action cannot fix the meaning of a word.[390] However, this anti-individualist reading requires particular interpretations of the words "practice" and "privately" that are not supported by the text. They read "practice" as "communal practice," whereas Wittgenstein's investigation of obeying a rule and the monologuists example shows that practice need not be communal. Further, they read "privately" as "individual," whereas the private linguist example shows that private does not mean individual, but rather dissociated from any behavior or activity.

The suggested alternate reading supports a coherent interpretation of the role of rules and private language in the broader argument of *Philosophical Investigations*. As we saw above, Wittgenstein's language-game picture alternative to the Augustinian view of language brings the concept of rules to the fore. Wittgenstein connects the discussion of rules and private language with a paradox. The paradox, he says, is "no course of action could be determined by a rule because every course of action can be made out to accord with the rule."[391] The paradox results if we assume that the rules which fix the meaning of our words require interpretation. Wittgenstein argues, instead, that while these rules guide our use of rules, we do not interpret them. They shape our world-picture and, thereby, how we see and act in the world. We are guided by rules insofar as they form the background of our judgments and beliefs.

The private language argument removes the final recourse for those who think we must interpret rules. Such thinkers, like Augustine, take it to be the case that learning language is learning how to translate our inner thoughts and experiences into the public language. They assume that we each have our own private language,

---

[390]Kripke (1982), 55, Malcolm (1988), 156.
[391]Wittgenstein (1967), §201.

completely dissociated from activity and understandable only to the individual. "The paradox," Wittgenstein says, "disappears only if we make a radical break with the idea that language always functions in one way, always serves the same purpose: to convey thoughts."[392] The private language argument is meant to show that the assumption underlying this view of language is a nonstarter. A private language is no language at all.

The suggestion of this reading of Wittgenstein on rules and private language is that activity is essential to meaning. Our rules have a determinate meaning because they shape our world-picture and, thereby, how we see and act in the world. The private language argument suggests that it is only insofar as our words are accompanied by activity that our words can have any meaning at all. In addition to being supported by particular passages in the text, this reading fits in with Wittgenstein's overall project in *Philosophical Investigations*. In introducing the term "language-game" Wittgenstein says, "the term 'language-game' is meant to bring into prominence the fact that the *speaking* of language is part of an activity, or a form of life."[393] What makes language meaningful is its relationship to how we live.

## WITTGENSTEIN AND THE NIETZSCHEAN INDIVIDUAL

The previous section provided an argument against anti-individualist readings of Wittgenstein on language. The foregoing reading of Wittgenstein on rules and private language favors Hacker's and Baker's reading of practices as regularities in behavior. According to this reading, only regularities of behavior—not collective or communal behavior or agreement—are conceptually required for language. This individualist

---

[392]Wittgenstein (1967), §304.

[393]Wittgenstein (1967), §23. Cf. "What has to be accepted, the given, is—so one could say—*forms of life*." Wittgenstein (1967), xi.

reading, however, fails to account for the important role the linguistic community plays with regard to the individual.

It is important to note that regularities in behavior are all that is *conceptually required* for language. Practically speaking, the picture is quite different. While communication may not be the essential function of language, conceptually speaking, communication is a highly important function of language, practically speaking. This fact has important implications for Wittgenstein. One of the underlying suggestions of Wittgenstein's *Philosophical Investigations* is that our shared language leads us to systematic confusions. Indeed, Wittgenstein says in a 1931 comment "Language sets everyone the same traps."[394] Wittgenstein focuses in particular on the traps in which analytic philosophers get stuck.

Though few miss Wittgenstein's interest in philosophical method, the implications of his thought for the individual are often overlooked. However, there are indications that he did not intend for these insights to be restricted to philosophers. In the *Philosophical Investigations*, he observes:

> The problems arising through a misinterpretation of our forms of language have the character of *depth*. They are deep disquietudes; their roots are as deep in us as the form of our language and their significance is as great as the importance of our language.[395]

These disquietudes are a feature of our common language. As such, they affect all speakers of that language. Thus, while his view of language has important implications for philosophers and the philosophical method, this is not the full extent of the ramifications of his philosophy. These insights also have implications for seemingly inevitable and irresolvable problems in the lay individual's life.

---

[394]Wittgenstein (1977), 18.
[395]Wittgenstein (1967), 111.

Indeed, comments not included in the *Philosophical Investigations* show Wittgenstein calling for something like the Nietzschean individual. Two such comments from 1937 show Wittgenstein concerned with a kind of culture crisis:

> . . . young people today can be said to be in a situation where ordinary common sense no longer suffices to meet the strange demands life makes. Everything has become so intricate that mastering it would require an exceptional intellect. Because skill at playing the game is no longer enough; the question that keeps coming up is: can this game be played at all now and what would be the right game to play?[396]

Here we see Wittgenstein applying the idea of games to the question of life in the early twentieth century. He suggests that the "game" of ordinary common sense may no longer be sufficient for the world in which people find themselves. The world has changed. It has become more complicated. As such, the game—the language-game—we share is no longer adequate to serve the needs of the individual.

Wittgenstein continues this topic with another comment from the same time period. He says:

> The way to solve the problem you see in life is to live in a way that will make what is problematic disappear.
>
> The fact that life is problematic shows that the shape of your life does not fit into life's mould. So you must change the way you live and, once your life does fit into the mould, what is problematic will disappear.[397]

The game of ordinary common sense is insufficient for life in the early twentieth century. Thus, the individual finds her life to be problematic. Wittgenstein suggests, just as we can resolve the problems of philosophy by doing philosophy differently, we can resolve the problems of life by living differently.

This theme reappears in 1946. In one such comment, Wittgenstein says:

---

[396]Wittgenstein (1977), 27e.
[397]Wittgenstein (1977), 27e.

> If life becomes hard to bear we think of a change in our circumstances. But the most important and effective change, a change in our own attitude, hardly ever occurs to us. And the resolution to take such a step is very difficult.[398]

The translation makes this sound like something out of a self-help book. Here, the German word "Verhalten" has been translated as "attitude," but it can also be translated as "behavior." This alternate translation is supported by a 1947 comment in which Wittgenstein likens a "Verhalten" to an "Art des Lebens" or a form of life.[399] If life becomes hard or problematic, Wittgenstein advises the individual to change her behavior or how she lives. The world-picture inherent in the shared language and form of life of her community is not sufficient to make sense of her life. She must, Wittgenstein says, find the strength to live in a different way.[400]

The stubborn communitarian may retort that these passages do nothing to show that Wittgenstein was concerned with the individual. When he advises a change in way of life, they may suggest, he is speaking to the collective or community. There's nothing to suggest otherwise. But there is. Wittgenstein sounds a thoroughly Nietzschean note in a 1944 comment. "That man," he says, "will be revolutionary who can revolutionize himself."[401] This comment is contemporaneous with the *Philosophical Investigations* and, thereby, with the collectivist's and communitarian's textual evidence.

According to the reading I've been developing, the individual can revolutionize herself if she changes the way she lives. As practice or regularity of behavior fixes meaning, a change in practice will change our words, language, and world-picture.

[398]Wittgenstein (1977), 53e.
[399]Wittgenstein (1977), 61.
[400]Cf. "Working in philosophy... is really more a working on oneself. On one's own interpretation. On one's own way of seeing things. (And what one expects of them.)" Wittgenstein (1977), 16e.
[401]Wittgenstein (1977), 45e.

What is needed is something like Millian experiments in living. Supposing the individual passes on her new way of life and language to others, such a change will literally change the world.[402] Communitarian thinkers, on the other hand, cannot even begin to account for this revolutionary Nietzschean comment.

The communitarian will retort that I cannot account for important passages in Wittgenstein's corpus. One such passage suggests that Wittgenstein envisioned a highly conservative role for philosophy:

> Philosophy may in no way interfere with the actual use of language; it can in the end only describe it.
> For it cannot give it any foundation either.
> It leaves everything as it is.[403]

Here Wittgenstein says that the role of philosophy is purely descriptive. Wittgenstein asserts that we cannot change meaning and thereby the world by philosophizing. But I take my reading to be consistent with this conservative role for philosophy. I am not suggesting that the individual can change meaning by engaging in the conceptual project of philosophizing. Rather, I am suggesting that the individual can change meaning by disrupting the regularities of behavior on which meaning depends. I am suggesting she live differently.

This section argued that language is not, conceptually speaking, essentially social. Language is social as a matter of fact. We share a common language and a world-picture. This common language sets us the same traps. In such cases, the fact that we share a common language can make these problems look inevitable and irresolvable. This is particularly problematic when our language and world-picture cease to be useful in making sense of the world in which we find ourselves. But these

---

[402]There's some very interesting work to be done here on the nature and dynamics of social movements.

[403]Wittgenstein (1967), §124.

problems are not inevitable or irresolvable. Wittgenstein calls on the individual to be something like the Nietzschean individual. The solution, Wittgenstein says, is to change how one lives.

This chapter was concerned with the suggestion that a Wittgensteinian view of language precludes the Nietzschean individual. An alternate reading of Wittgenstein on rules and private language was offered according to which activity, not community behavior or consensus, is necessary for meaning. This alternate reading, however, does not embrace the full-blown individualist reading of Hacker and Baker. The fact is that our linguistic community plays an important role in our experience. Our shared language leads us into the same traps. The fact that we share this language makes the resulting problems appear inevitable and irresolvable.

Wittgenstein once remarked that he didn't wish to found a school of philosophy. This reading suggests an explanation. His philosophy was a response to a culturally troubled time. The world had changed such that the form of life individuals had been given by society no longer met the demands of their lives. They experienced their lives as deeply problematic. Like Nietzsche, Wittgenstein rejects the view that these problems are inevitable and irresolvable. Their source lies in our language and culture. Their solution is the Nietzschean individual, that individual with the courage to live differently. Wittgenstein didn't want to found a school, then, because he hoped his philosophy would show us how to remove the problems that motivated it. The next chapter will return to the question of the fate of our individual caught in moment of culture crisis.

## CULTURE CRISIS REVISITED

This thesis was concerned with the phenomenon of culture crisis. In particular, this thesis asked whether there was anything the individual could do to resolve the problem of culture crisis in her own case. Initially, I characterized culture crisis as a historical moment in which our culture comes apart from the practical realties of our lives. In a moment of culture crisis our culture suddenly and radically no longer helps us to make sense of the world in which we find ourselves. Our culture leads us to expect one world, but we find ourselves in another.

In order to illustrate the problem of culture crisis, I used Generation Y's experience as an example. The 2008 Recession and its fall-out have indelibly and irreversibly altered Generation Y's experience. As I argued in the first chapter, Generation Y expected to find itself in the world of Dilbert or Leslie Knope. Comparison of the films from 1999 and the television shows from 2009 shows that Generation Y had begun to accept the bureau as the non-threatening background of their lives. Generation Y's picture of the good life took for granted that they would have a place within a bureau and would be able to live modest and comfortable, if sometimes absurd lives.

The fall-out of the 2008 Recession has made this picture of the good life unattainable. The members of Generation Y have adapted the picture to account for some of the financial setbacks they've experienced. They are putting off getting married, buying houses, having kids and even simply buying a car. However, these adaptations, importantly, do not question the essential features of the good life.

Supposing the economy fails to return to something resembling its pre-Recession state, this light adaptation will not be enough.

The culture crisis facing Generation Y threatens to doom its members to living unfulfilled and unsatisfied lives. They remain in the grips of a pre-Recession picture of the good life, but live in a post-Recession world. What the members of Generation Y need is a picture of the good life that can help them navigate the post-Recession world. Given that culture is a collective creation, the problem of culture crisis ultimately requires a collective solution. However, collective solutions take time whereas the individual has a life to live right now. This thesis asked if there was anything the individual could to do resolve this problem in her own case.

I argued in the second chapter that we need something like a Wittgensteinian view of language to even make sense of the phenomenon of culture crisis. According to this view, language is not an instrument of science. Rather, language is an activity. Our concepts get their meaning from their relation to our activities or form of life. Taken as a whole, our concepts form a world-picture which is the socially inherited background of our judgements and beliefs. It shapes how we see and act in the world.

On a Wittgensteinian understanding of language, many of our concepts are unbounded and governed by indefinite rules. Generally, we follow the rules of our language easily. However, Wittgenstein suggests that we sometimes get trapped or entangled in the rules of our language. We try to use our concepts in accordance with their rules, but things do not go as we expect them to. In such cases we tend to look for the problem in the wrong place. That is, we often fail to consider that our concepts are the source of the problem.

The unbounded nature of our concepts on the Wittgensteinian view means that the rules governing them take for granted certain normal conditions. If these conditions no longer hold, then the concept will no longer work as expected. This is a reasonable explanation of the problem facing Generation Y. The pre-Recession picture of the good life takes certain conditions for granted. These conditions include things such as a growing economy and an abundance of mid-wage jobs, for instance. However, these conditions no longer obtain in the post-Recession world. The pre-Recession picture of the good life is, therefore, no longer a good concept.

If this is a good analysis of the problem facing Generation Y, then the solution lies in concept revision or creation. I argued in the third and fourth chapters that the Nietzschean individual provides a model for our individual caught in a moment of culture crisis. In the third chapter I gave a physio-psychological reading of Nietzsche's work according to which the decline of culture in late nineteenth century Europe is a result of declining physio-psychological health. Broadly, the problem Nietzsche sees is that the culture of late nineteenth century Europe does not help individuals make sense of their lives. Rather than providing them ways to endure and embrace the suffering that characterizes life, their culture denies that life involves suffering. The solution to this cultural problem is the self-overcoming Nietzschean individual.

In the fourth chapter I examined the notion of overcoming. As the Nietzschean individual is supposed to carry out a cultural revival via self-overcoming, the notion of overcoming is central to Nietzsche's project. I argued that a coherent and non-metaphorical understanding of overcoming rests on Nietzsche's neglected and underdeveloped view of language. According to this view, we give form and order to ourselves and the world via the creation and application of concepts. Nietzsche characterizes our concepts as an interpretation of our experience, especially our physio-psychological experience. The interpretation we create is driven by power struggles between different segments of society and enforced through moral imperative. Nonetheless, Nietzsche believes all concepts, not just the moral, are human interpretations which give form and order to our diverse and multidudinous experience.

The Nietzschean individual, then, is supposed to carry out a cultural revival by engaging in concept revision and creation. She is supposed to give a new interpretation. Realizing that concepts are a human creation, the Nietzschean individual does not remain passively within the confines of the concepts she was given, but rather realizes her nature as a creative animal and overcomes. She rejects the collective form of life and is, thereby, able to generate new concepts.

I suggested at the end of the fourth chapter that Nietzsche's view of language shares its central insight with Wittgenstein's view. In the fifth chapter I considered the challenge that a Wittgensteinian view of language precludes the Nietzschean individual. This challenge rests upon a collectivist or communitarian reading of Wittgenstein on language and rules. Such readings hold that language is essentially social and the individual is insufficient to determine meaning for herself. As such, the individual cannot engage in concept revision and creation. I argued that this reading is unsupported by the text. According to Wittgenstein, regularity in activity is necessary for meaning, not collective or communal agreement in behavior. Indeed, Wittgenstein even seems to call for the Nietzschean individual.

The overall suggestion of this thesis, then, is that to resolve the problem of culture crisis in her own case, the individual needs to be like the Nietzschean individual. Once she has recognized that the problem facing her is that her picture or concept of the good life is not longer a good one, she must overcome and, thereby, give herself a new concept. This suggestion is unlikely to find many sympathetic ears as traditional interpretation suggests that the thought of these thinkers is either irrelevant to incompatible with each other.

However, the suggestion of the fourth and fifth chapters is that Wittgenstein's and Nietzsche's work is not incompatible or even radically different. Rather, they were both concerned with the question of cultural decline, its sources, symptoms, and solution. Both thinkers appeal to the individual, trying to shake her free of the picture or perspective that holds her captive. Nietzsche employed his talent to articulate the problem of culture and identified overcoming as the solution. Wittgenstein employed his talent to explore the nature of language and saw that something like his view of language was necessary to make sense of this problem and its solution.

This commonality in purpose explains certain aspects of these thinkers' works. If Wittgenstein was concerned with culture and the human condition, as this comparison suggests, then we can make sense of his frequent comments regarding religion, war, progress, and culture. Additionally, this helps us make sense of the ethical dimension of the *Tractatus*. As Bearn suggests, Wittgenstein saw an intimate connection between the nature of language and the human condition. This thesis suggests that this connection remains in his later thought as well. On the other hand, comparing Nietzsche with Wittgenstein helps resolve long-standing interpretive issues regarding his views on language, truth, and overcoming.

With these sources of incompatibility out of the way, the individual is free to resolve the problem of culture crisis in her own case. The problem of culture crisis is a conceptual problem. It is an instance of conceptual failure. The pre-Recession concept of the good life is no longer a good one because the normal conditions it takes for granted no longer obtain. Though the problem of culture crisis is conceptual, its solution is not. The solution, as Wittgenstein suggests is to change how one lives.

Our individual must create a new or significantly revised form of life to serve as the basis of a revised language and world-picture.

It is important to note, however, that this is not meant to be a solution to be a universal solution to the problem facing Generation Y. The aim of this thesis is much more limited. The question was whether there is anything *the individual* can do to resolve the problem *in her own case*. The suggestion coming out of this thesis is that there is. Even so, not every individual member of Generation Y will be able to pursue this solution because it requires the individual be both a philosopher and a Nietzschean individual. That is, the individual must both be able to recognize the conceptual nature of the problem and also have the strength of will to live differently. This is an exceedingly rare individual.

The solution to the problem facing Generation Y as a whole, then, does not lie immediately in the process of overcoming. This is something that the rare individual undertakes. However, as I suggested in the third chapter, Nietzsche believed these individuals would have a profound and far-reaching effect upon culture and the world. The world, he said, "revolves about the inventor of new values: imperceptibly it revolves."[404] He is, characteristically, not explicit about what he means by this. However, I think it likely that he imagines the Nietzschean individual to be something like a tastemaker. They set an example through their way of living which others imitate. The imitators' actions themselves have knock-on effects. The Nietzschean individual's actions, thereby, initiate a cultural revival.

The conclusion of this thesis is cautiously optimistic. It is, conceptually speaking, possible for the individual to resolve the problem of culture crisis in her own case. The members of Generation Y are not, necessarily, fated to live unsatisfied

---

[404]Nietzsche (1969), 78.

and unfulfilling lives because they remain in the grips of a pre-Recession picture of the good life. However, the individuals with the ability to develop a picture of the good life better suited to the post-Recession world are exceedingly rare. Despite this conceptual possibility, then, the majority of Generation Y are likely fated to pretend that the pre-Recession picture of the good life is still a good picture.

# BIBLIOGRAPHY

Ansell-Pearson, Keith. *An Introduction to Nietzsche as Political Thinker: The Perfect Nihilist.* Cambridge University Press, 1994.

Baker, Gordon, and Peter Hacker. *Scepticism, Rules and Language.* Blackwell, 1984.

———. "Malcolm on Language and Rules." *Philosophy* 65, 252: (1990) 167–179.

Bearn, Gordon. *Waking to Wonder: Wittgenstein's Existential Investigations.* State University of New York Press, 1997.

Bloor, David. *Wittgenstein: A Social Theory of Knowledge.* Macmillan, 1983.

———. *Wittgenstein, Rules and Institutions.* Routledge, 1997.

———. "Ludwig Wittgenstein and Edmund Burke." In *Essays on Wittgenstein and Austrian Philosophy: in honor of J.C. Nyíri,* edited by Tamas Demeter, Rodopi, 2004, 109–136.

Candlish, Stewart. "The Real Private Language Argument." *Philosophy* 55, 211: (1980) 85–94.

Canfield, John. "The Community View." *The Philosophical Review* 105, 4: (1996) 469–488.

Carr, Craig. *Polity: Political Culture and the Nature of Politics.* Rowman & Littlefield Publishers, Inc., 2007.

Cerbone, David. "The Limits of Conservatism: Wittgenstein on 'Our Life' and 'Our Concepts'." In *The Grammar of Politics: Wittgenstein and Political Philosophy,* edited by Cressida Heyes, Cornell University Press, 2003, 43–62.

Clark, Maudemarie. *Nietzsche on Truth and Philosophy.* Cambridge University Press, 1990.

Conway, Daniel. *Nietzsche and the Political.* Routledge, 1996.

Crary, Alice. "Wittgenstein's Philosophy in Relation to Political Thought." In *The New Wittgenstein,* edited by Alice Crary, and Rupert Read, Routledge, 2000, 118–141.

Danto, Arthur. *Nietzsche as Philosopher.* Columbia University Press, 2005.

Diamond, Cora. "Ethics, Imagination and the Method of Wittgenstein's *Tractatus.*" In *The New Wittgenstein*, edited by Alice Crary, and Rupert Read, Routledge, 2000, 149–173.

Hacker, Peter. "Wittgenstein, Carnap and the New American Wittgensteinians." *The Philosophical Quarterly* 53, 210: (2003) 1–23.

———. "Robinson Crusoe Sails Again: The Interpretative Relevance of Wittgenstein's *Nachlass.*" In *Wittgenstein After His Nachlass*, edited by Nuno Venturinha, Palgrave Macmillan, 2010, 91–109.

Heller, Erich. "Wittgenstein and Nietzsche." In *The Artist's Journey into the Interior, and Other Essays*, Harcourt Brace Jovanvich, 1976, 201–226.

Kaufmann, Walter. *Nietzsche: Philosopher, Psychologist, Antichrist.* Princeton University Press, 1950.

Kripke, Saul. *Wittgenstein on Rules and Private Language: An Elementary Exposition.* Harvard University Press, 1982.

Malcolm, Norman. "Moore and Ordinary Language." In *Ordinary Language: Essays in Philosophical Method*, edited by V.C. Chappell, Dover Publications, 1981, 5–23.

———. *Wittgenstein: Nothing is Hidden.* Blackwell, 1988.

———. "Wittgenstein on Language and Rules." *Philosophy* 64, 247: (1989) 5–28.

McManus, Denis. *The Enchantment of Words: Wittgenstein's "Tractatus Logico-Philosophicus".* Oxford University Press, 2006.

MGMT. ""Time to Pretend"." In *Oracular Spectacular*, Sony Music, 2008. Sound recording.

Monk, Ray. *Ludwig Wittgenstein: Duty of Genius.* Macmillan, 1990.

Nietzsche, Friedrich. "The Anti-Christ." Penguin Books Ltd., 1968a.

———. "Twilight of the Idols." Penguin Books Ltd., 1968b.

———. *Thus Spoke Zarathustra.* Penguin Books Ltd., 1969.

———. "On Truth and Lies in a Nonmoral Sense." In *Philosophy and Truth: Selections from Nietzsche's Notebooks of the early 1870's*, edited by Daniel, Huma, 1979, 79–97.

———. "Beyond Good and Evil." In *Basic Writings of Nietzsche*, edited by Walter Kaufmann, Modern Library, 1992a.

———. "On the Genealogy of Morals." In *Basic Writings of Nietzsche*, edited by Walter Kaufmann, Modern Library, 1992b.

Nyíri, János. "Wittgenstein's Later Work in Relation to Conservatism." In *Wittgenstein in His Times*, Thoemmes, 1998.

Owen, David. *Nietzsche, Politics & Modernity: A Critique of Liberal Reason.* Sage Publishing, 1995.

———. "Nietzsche, Enlightment and the Problem of Noble Ethics." In *Nietzsche's Futures*, Macm, 1999.

———. "Wittgenstein and Genealogy." *Nordic Journal of Philosophy* 2, 2: (2001) 5–29.

———. "Criticism and Captivity: On Genealogy and Critical Theory." *European Journal of Philosophy* 10, 2: (2002) 216–230.

———. "Genealogy as Perspicuous Representation." In *The Grammar of Politics: Wittgenstein and Political Philosophy*, edited by Cressida Heyes, Cornell University Press, 2003, 82–96.

Pears, David. *Wittgenstein.* Fontana Press, 1985.

———. *The False Prison: A Study of the Development of Wittgenstein's Philosophy*, volume Two. Oxford University Press, 1988.

Pippin, Robert. "How to Overcome Oneself: Nietzsche on Freedom." In *Nietzsche on Freedom and Autonomy*, edited by Ken Gemes, and Simon May, Oxford University Press, 2009, 69–87.

———. *Nietzsche, Psychology & First Philosophy.* Chicago University Press, 2010.

Pitkin, Hanna. *Wittgenstein and Justice: On the Significance of Ludwig Wittgenstein for Social and Political Thought.* University of California Press, 1972.

Robinson, Christopher. *Wittgenstein and Political Theory: The View from Somewhere.* Edinburgh University Press, 2009.

Rundle, Bede. "The Private Language Argument." In *Wittgenstein and Analytic Philosophy: Essays for P.M.S. Hacker*, edited by Hans Johann Glock, and John Hyman, Oxford University Press, 2009, 133–151.

Russell, Bertrand. "Knowledge by Acquaintance and Knowledge by Description." *Proceedings of the Aristotelian Society* 11: (1910-1911) 108–128.

Sluga, Hans. *Wittgenstein*. Wiley-Blackwell, 2011.

Sontag, Frederick. *Wittgenstein and the Mystical: Philosophy as an Ascetic Practice*. Scholars Press, 1995.

Szabados, Béla. *Ludwig Wittgenstein on Race, Gender and Cultural Identity: Philosophy as a Personal Endeavor*. Edwin Mellen Press, 2010.

de Tocqueville, Alexis. *Democracy in America*. Harper & Row, 1969.

Winch, Peter. *The Idea of a Social Science and its Relation to Philosophy*. Routledge & Kegan Paul Ltd., 1973.

Wittgenstein, Ludwig. *The Blue and Brown Books: Preliminary Studies for the "Philosophical Investigations"*. Basil Blackwell, 1958.

———. *Tractatus Logico-Philosophicus*. Routledge & Kegan Paul Ltd., 1961.

———. "A Lecture on Ethics." *The Philosophical Review* 74, 1: (1965) 3–12.

———. *Philosophical Investigations*. Basil Blackwell, 1967.

———. *On Certainty*. Basil Blackwell, 1969.

———. *Culture and Value*. Basil Blackwell, 1977.

von Wright, Georg. "Wittgenstein in Relation to His Times." In *Wittgenstein and His Times*, edited by Brian McGuinness, Thoemmes, 1998, 108–120.